To Ride a Rocking Horse

By Roger Daniel

To Ride A Rocking Horse

ISBN-13: 978-1456539092

TORIDEAROCKINGHORSE.COM

Also by Roger Daniel

Detour
(How Did I Get Where I Am After I Mapped Out My Life So Well)

ISBN-13: 978-1456472764

THEBOOKDETOUR.COM

Acknowledgements

I want to thank all the law enforcement officers who were part of the investigation and responsible for brining this case to trial. With their professional work, knowledge of the law, and long hours working on this case, the convictions were possible. Their thoroughness in compiling evidence assured that the case held up through the appeals process. Many times they helped me complete my story by giving me information they had not shared with other reporters.

Also deserving recognition are the attorneys for the State and defense who were always available for comments during and after the trial. No matter how the trial was unfolding on any given day, the attorneys on both sides were courteous to me and my photographer. Even when they were being pressed for quotes by me and the many reporters who descended upon them at every break in the trial they took the time to answer all the questions fired at them while in the heat and bright glare of multiple television camera lights.

And I give special thanks to the photographers who helped me edit my tapes, got soundbites for me, and made sure we had enough video to put together a story every day. This was possible because they did the heavy work of carrying the camera and battery packs in the courthouse, as well as the strenuous job of shooting video in the most sweltering and humid part of a Southeast Texas summer.

CHAPTER ONE

Perfect Planning for the Perfect Crime

It was perfect. Perfect. Everything was perfect. If they had brought the guns they could kill them right then. As the two of them lay in the grass outside the house they could almost reach out and touch Bishop and Ester. They hid in the grass and watched his former in-laws eat supper and then get up and move to the living room to watch TV. They could hear what they were saying. They could see and hear their movements in the house. They could almost hear their thoughts. This was going to be so easy he wanted to laugh. He wanted to laugh at them for all the times they made his life miserable. He wanted to laugh at them for sitting there so unconcerned when he was going to break in and kill them as easy as saying, "Hi, Bishop. Hi Ester. Remember me? It's payback time."

He was never a good student in school. The only recognition he ever got was as a troublemaker. Although he never scored very well in school he was scoring an A+, 100%, perfect, that night. He was lying there in the grass completely overtaken by his brilliance. It was planned down to the smallest detail, including packing a bottle of mosquito repellant. They did not want any sounds of slapping mosquitoes to foil their sneak attack. And they sure did not want any big red welts from mosquito bites to raise suspicion that they might have recently been out in the night.

Phase One was the planning. This night was Phase Two, the night of the dress rehearsal. This was the night they put on their fatigues, blackened their faces, and practiced their attack strategy on Bishop and Ester's house. Phase One, perfect. Phase Two, perfect. It was all working to perfection. He was beginning to get the feeling nothing could go wrong. He felt invincible.

The area around the Phillips's home in Southeast Texas is mostly rice farms. Every year Winnie, a little town on the interstate between Houston and Louisiana, hosts the biggest rice festival in Texas. One part of growing rice is flooding the fields. Rice can grow in water, weeds cannot. If the fields around their house had been flooded it would have served as a moat, providing the Phillips family with more protection from the planned sneak attack.

But it was not rice; it was another grain crop growing around the Phillips's house. No flooded fields, no short stalks of rice were growing near their house. Instead corn, that stands about five feet tall by late June in Texas, was beginning to fill out under the blistering Texas sun. The ground was dry making sure footing for anyone coming down the corn rows. The corn hid the Phillips's house from view in every direction except from the front which faced the road. There were several trees and bushes in the yard that partially obscured that view too.

He and his girlfriend had noticed the corn earlier when they drove by to make a complete layout of the house and the fields around it. They saw they would only have a few feet to actually creep up on the house. They could walk through the corn. The corn would hide them until they came out of the field into the yard. The corn still had some green to it, which would help muffle the sound of their approach and make their advance on the house easier. Green corn leaves are softer than dry corn, making it much less likely to leave any telltale cut marks on them.

Everything was perfect. After that night's rehearsal they would be back on the July fourth weekend. If anything happened on the weekend of the 4th that did not go with the plans, no problem, they would kill them right there. Who would notice? A few pops on the Fourth of July weekend, big deal, just fireworks nobody would pay any attention to for even an instant.

The daring and brilliance of the plan excited him. His heart was pounding and he was ready to kill the Phillips right then. It was all he could do to keep from jumping up, kicking in the door and with a huge smirk on his face bust in with guns blazing. But seeing how easy it would be, he could also feel that by waiting, savoring the joy, the revenge, and the thrill of killing them he could make the event last much longer than if they went in and did it right then. But most important, that was not part of the plan. It had to be on the Fourth of July weekend.

His girlfriend lay beside him in the grass. She was not laughing. She was not basking in his brilliance. She was studying Bishop and Ester, watching their movements, paying attention to how they interacted and reacted to things that came up. There was no hatred in her for the Phillips. For her it was something to do. It was a challenge. If you planned it all out and then executed the plan to perfection it could even be enjoyable. For her this time was for thinking, not gloating. She watched for details. She knew she needed to keep her wits about her if this was going to work.

He was hot-headed. He had a flash temper that could make a shambles of the best-laid plans. She knew him well enough to know she not only had to worry about the plans, she had to worry about him. She did not question if he had the viciousness to carry out the attack. She questioned his nerve. She had been honky-tonking with him and knew bartenders all over the Port Arthur area hated to see him walk through the door because it was almost a guarantee there would be a brawl before the night was over. He was constantly in trouble for fighting but she knew he was rarely lying around licking his wounds afterwards. She had seen him in action for herself and knew he never fought a fair fight so there were seldom any wounds to heal. And she knew when the two of them broke through the door with guns in their hands; this would not be a fair fight either.

He was a big, burly, brawny, bull of a man. The weak point in his makeup was at the top of that young, muscular body was the mind of a frightened child. A child that cringed from the physical and mental abuse he had suffered when he was young. He saw the world as a place where he had to constantly be on guard because someone was always trying to hurt him. He fought back with force like a man, but only when the opponents were much smaller. He was a man out to whip the world, to return some of those whippings he got as a child. He always looked for a situation where he was the larger person, the adult, giving the whipping to someone smaller who needed to be straightened out and taught to act like he thought they should.

She was nearly a hundred pounds lighter than him but she had total control of him and the situation. Part of that control was sex. That was how their relationship began. She was in and out of bars several nights a week while her second husband stayed home with her kids.

His favorite bars were the ones of Southeast Texas that played the genuine, real thing, swamp-water fais-do-do Acadian music. He was not a Cajun, or "coonass" as they are more often called in the Port Arthur area, but he liked their distinctive dancing and sound of the zydeco accordion. The most authentic night-spot for that was the Rodair Club on Highway 365. With his taste for music, it was inevitable that his path and hers would cross. Both were searching for "Laissez Les Bons Temps Rouler," French for "let the good times roll." It was not long before they were letting the good times roll to where they usually wind up when you are out honky tonkin' instead of being at home with your spouse and kids.

The rest of the control she had over him was her nerve. She weighed less than a hundred pounds but larger persons or odds did not bother her. She knew how to turn the odds in her favor. She could do it through ways such as, first, find a guy long on macho bravado but short on guts. She could supply the guts. She had the nerve, he had the brawn. The bigger and stronger he thought he was and the easier to control, the better it was for her. His resume fit the bill perfectly. He was her evil dream come true.

He liked fighting and he liked coonass music. His dream job came along when the Rodair Club hired him as a bouncer. He made a good one except that he became a bigger problem than the trouble makers. He was bouncing a little too often, almost every time someone significantly smaller than himself walked through the door.

And there was another problem. He would not just bounce a patron. He would get them outside the club and beat them far beyond the call of duty as a bouncer. It was after the club got its first lawsuit from one of his over-zealous bouncings that he got bounced from his job. After the manager of the Rodair Club fired him he still came back to hang out and to fight without the club's sponsorship.

Only once did he get into a fight and find himself in serious trouble. One night a small, slight built man came into the club. Sizing him up as an easy mark, he quickly singled him out as another opportunity to prove his toughness. What he did not know was that the guy was a black belt in Karate. It was one night he went home severely bruised and bleeding.

For him the most important part of being the toughest man in Southeast Texas was not to just be feared by every bar patron in the area, but to be envied by them. If you want other men to envy you, you have to have a woman. For a single guy, a married woman is an even bigger trophy. She was his trophy. She validated his credentials as a guy to be feared and envied. His old lady was somebody else's old lady. She was his message to all the men that neither their bodies nor their wives were safe when he was around. She was his certificate to swagger.

After lying there for almost an hour she whispered in his ear, "It's perfect. Let's go. It's gettin' late. Let's make sure we leave exactly like we come in. We can retrace our steps and double check the route in and out to make sure it don't have no flaws. Let's go back down the corn row so we don't leave no footprints. We don't want nothin' to tip them off. We don't want them gettin' suspicious of nothin'."

When they were back in their car and had driven away from the house they were both on an adrenalin high. Everything worked to perfection. It was going to be so easy that they laughed and joked about it.

"Boy there's gonna be two old farts with their eyeballs popping out of their heads when they see us comin' through the door in camouflage and their noses stuck down the barrel of a gun. They'll be so scared they might just fire off a shot or two themselves ... in their pants," she bragged to him as she rolled back her head and laughed at the shock that would be registered on their faces. She knew the plan was perfect and they would take them completely by surprise.

"Yep. I can't tell you how good that's going to make me feel," he said, "but it still won't even the score. Not until they're in that hole in the ground."

They were on a high and everything was working out perfectly. Only one thing could make the night any better. They took care of that in the back seat of his car once they got back to the Rodair Club.

CHAPTER TWO

Five Phillips Family Members Are Missing

"Damn it's hot," I mumbled and cursed to myself as I walked from my car to the back door of the station. The concrete in the parking lot was beginning to radiate heat and it was nine o'clock in the morning. The temperature and the humidity were well into the 80's. It was one of those mornings when your photographer has to take the camera outside for about five minutes to acclimatize so it will not fog up.

Bringing a camera right out of the air conditioned building in the morning into the heat and humidity meant condensation on all your equipment. Do that and it means foggy video at best or a destroyed video tape in the worst case scenario. That then brings the wrath of an assignment editor, news director, and news anchor down upon you when the whole newscast has to be revamped to fill the hole created by your lost story.

I was born in Texas and had spent almost thirty summers there but I still was not comfortable with the overpowering heat and humidity that starts in early spring and ends in late fall. On top of that, it was a Monday morning and I had five straight mornings like this to look forward to before the weekend.

"Jay's loading up the camera gear now. I want you guys to go down to a farmhouse in Winnie," the assignment editor greeted me as I walked through the door.

That is the way it is in news. When time is of essence your greeting when walking through the door is not always "Good morning!" Sometimes it is sentence fragments. They are fragments that give you parts of journalism's basic who, what, where, when and why. The "when" is always "Now." Sometimes you do not even get that much. Sometimes they just tell you to get in the news unit and go. You get directions to where you are going and why you're going on the way to your assignment.

"Five members of a family out in rural Winnie have disappeared," Ted, the assignment editor, said as I was digging through my desk looking for my notebook. "The sheriff's office thinks there might be foul play. Lights were on, a platter of chicken was sitting on the table, the coffee pot was on and coffee scorched on the bottom, and nobody's seen the five of them for 3 days. It sounds highly improbable they went somewhere without coercion because 3 of them were visiting from Oklahoma. They had no plans to go anywhere or do anything. They just came down to spend the weekend of the fourth with their family in Winnie," Ted added, trying to arm me with a few facts before I took off for Winnie, about thirty minutes away from Beaumont.

"Even more odd," Ted added, "is that the old man is a diabetic and has to have regular medication. They went off and left that. Wherever they are, he needs his medication. If he doesn't get it soon, he could die. So it doesn't sound too likely that they just left the house to go to the beach or some other place."

"Where's the house? Who are we talking about?" I said trying to get a few basics before I left. I did not want to have to use the two-way radio and call in halfway there. If any of the other stations hadn't picked up on the story yet saying the wrong thing on the radio would tip them off.

"It's the family of Bishop and Ester Phillips. The house is on farm to market road fourteen-oh-six. It's about 3 miles north of Interstate ten," Ted advised me. "There may be sheriff's deputies around the house doing more investigating. Get us some kind of visuals and some sound bites from anybody who'll talk."

There were no sheriff's deputies when Jay and I arrived. In spite of that we had no trouble finding the house. There were 3 news units from radio and television stations already there along with two private cars of newspaper reporters sent out to get pictures and talk to authorities. A short time later there was a film crew from a station in Houston, more than an hour away from Winnie.

Winnie is in the northeastern corner of Chambers County, and that summer the domain of Sheriff Doyle Pounds. In any other summer the biggest excitement this time of the year would have been when the deputies pulled traffic duty at the rice festival. That involves directing traffic for the tens of thousands of cars that pull through the gates as Southeast Texans gather to celebrate the harvesting of the rice crop at the annual Winnie Rice Festival. It is long hours for the officers, but it is easy and enjoyable work that is a break from their normal routine patrol duty and brings them overtime pay. Best of all, there is none of the lawman's most dreaded crime-fighting chore - paperwork.

The events at the Phillips's home were about to change all of that for this summer. If the five missing people did not show up somewhere, the small, rural sheriff's department had a mass murder on their hands. Five murders in a decade would constitute a crime wave in Winnie. Five murders in one weekend would be talked about for generations.

The heat was even worse by the time we got to the farm house. All the media was huddled under shade trees trying to escape the sun's building intensity. That, along with the house being small, made it impossible to get any wide shots of the place without getting another camera crew or reporter in your picture.

The house was a small wood frame that looked like Bishop

Phillips had seen more bad years as a farmer than good ones. It needed a little paint to spruce up the outside and about a thousand more square feet of floor space to make the interior more livable. It did not look like much and the lack of air conditioning units in the windows made you wonder how Bishop and Ester had lived there and raised their family in it through more than 3 decades of steamy Texas summers.

I did not know a whole lot when I got there, which put me on even footing with all the other reporters.

"Hey, they've got some really juicy looking rabbits in the hutch out back," Wayne Sparrow from Channel Six said, announcing the first bit of information anyone was able to uncover. "I might come back after dark if no one's here. There are some prime candidates for barbecuing back there."

It was that kind of day and that kind of story. All we had for video was exteriors of a small, shaded farmhouse. A few pictures and a quick trip around the house doing the elementary detective work every reporter does when sent to cover a crime story. That was it. The only thing that moved in the stifling heat was the minimal shuffling of the rabbits and the photographers trying every angle possible to get enough video to make a minute and a half news story. There was no breeze in the trees or moving through the field of corn next to the house. Since there was officially no crime, we all wanted to get as many pictures from as many angles as possible, get an interview with a law officer, and get back to meet a deadline, or just get back to the air conditioned station. We also knew to get as much video as possible, because even with a happy ending, this was a story that was going to be part of every newscast for days.

"See if you can get a shot through the kitchen window, or through one of the windows to give us some kind of glimpse into the inside. You know, to make the viewers feel like we're putting them in the middle of the crime scene. And to give us some file video in case it really turns out to be a crime," I suggested to Jay, who was standing there with the camera on his shoulder and frustration on his face.

"No way. I've been all around the house. All the shades are drawn, the windows are shut, and the doors locked. The sheriff's department has entirely sealed it off. What you see out here is all you're going to see," said Jay, a seasoned photographer and obviously about five minutes ahead of me on ideas for video.

"So what do we do?" I was fishing for his input on how to put together a story on something that sounded very suspicious but at that point could have been five persons taking off for a weekend out of town. Maybe they decided to drive the hour trip into Houston to go to Astroworld and did not think it necessary to tell anyone where they had gone. Maybe they just headed for the beach to escape the heat and get some barbecued crabs at Sartin's in Sabine Pass.

"I could get a low shot of the road," Jay suggested. "That would give a picture accentuating the length of the road and how far the house is from town or any neighbors. It's just a thought, but right now we need some thoughts because I sure don't have much video to support the story."

"We've got a house, which isn't moving," Jay said taking a video inventory. "We've got a few shots of the trees and bushes around the house, which also are not moving. For the video part of the story, we're hurting. Other than a talking head this is basically going to be a story of still pictures. I can get a little artsy with camera angles but I sure can't give it any pizzazz."

I did not have any pizzazz with the words either. It was an interesting story but with no victims, no suspects, and so far, no crime, it was just a "what if" story. I hated "what if" stories where the reporter spends a minute an a half saying, "There's no story here we can substantiate, but boy oh boy, "what if" something really has happened? Wouldn't that be an exciting news story folks?" To me "what if" stories had the sincerity of hucksterism. "We don't really have a news story folks, but "what if" we had admitted that up front and you switched to another channel? So to keep you tuned to our station, I'll just speculate for a minute and a half." I have seen it on TV many times, saw through it every time, and highly suspected the viewers do as well.

"What if" something happened to these people? "What if" there was foul play?" Or worse, "What if" they all showed up before the newscast and my story went down the dumper leaving a minute-thirty hole in the newscast?

The other "what if" was what if a day or a week later the sheriff discovers something really bad happened to these people and we did not tell our viewers about it. That was the only "what if" that was certain. It is either a story on the air tonight, or egg on your face tomorrow.

We got a slight reprieve and bit of hope when a pickup pulled into the driveway with a sheriff's deputy behind the wheel. At last, something moving, even if it was just a deputy pulling in and out of the driveway.

The focal point of all the reporters and cameras quickly shifted to the truck and the deputy. Only the photographers got anything usable. The deputy rolled down his window to say he was looking for other law officers and had nothing to say for the record or even for a "don't quote me" attribute. When he discovered the officers were not there, he started to leave. I watched as Wayne, who was now more interested in the deputy than the best way to barbecue rabbits, jumped up on the running board of the pickup and tried to get some tiny scrap of news, anything at all to add some substance to the story.

It was a relief to see that in spite of Wayne's intrusion the deputy kept backing out of the drive. A reporter in his face was not enough to stop the camera-shy deputy from quickly leaving the scene. Wayne saw the camera fright in the deputy's eyes and realized he would be quite content to just drive off with a reporter dangling from his truck. Holding on to his reporter's notebook and the pickup, Wayne finally jumped off before the deputy got out into the road and took off. It was good to know he did not get a quote or some inside information making his story better than mine.

Wayne did not get his story angle, but he did make everyone else at the scene angry. It was the only moving object that morning, and he ruined it for everyone by sticking his head into the driver's side window and hanging his butt squarely in the middle of every photographer's picture frame. By putting all of his body in the driver's window he also prevented any radio reporter getting a microphone in the window for a quote.

"Okay, what do we do now?" I asked Jay, who was huffing from trying to get out in the road and get a shot of the disappearing truck. "It's pretty evident nothing's going to happen here."

"Go to the Sheriff's office?" Jay suggested.

"I guess so. We can't drive the thirty miles back to the station with what little we've got so far. Let's go into town. The Sheriff's office will have to say something because all the media from Houston to Lake Charles, Louisiana, are now on the story. We can find a phone and see what the station has uncovered from their end," I said surveying our limited options.

As I looked at my watch my thoughts turned to my stomach. "It's close to noon," I said thinking of how to put a positive spin on the situation. "We can get some fried alligator for lunch at Al T's. If they're out, we can eat crawfish. This could be a good story after all. Maybe we'll get sent back enough to have the gator and the mud bugs, and if we're really lucky, Friday's Cajun gumbo."

The thought of going into town was not just my attention turning to my stomach. Going into Winnie also meant back in the air conditioned car and out of the stifling heat. I was ready for the inside part of the story, going to the sheriff's department and talking to the sheriff or a newly anointed public relations officer serving as a buffer between the sheriff and the news media. Either way, I got my air conditioned interview, I got something of substance to make a story, and I confidently knew I got just as much at the scene as any other reporter covering the story.

While in Winnie I began writing the story in my mind. It

was past noon and the clock ticking towards news time. I was nervous about getting a story together but confident I could pull together enough for a minute-thirty report. All I needed was a quote from somebody and I knew I would have one before we left town. I would find a willing participant at the sheriff's office, or back at the station Ted would find me a quotable person by making some phone calls. My story was shaping up -- thick on intrigue but thin on facts -- neatly wrapped up and ready for a minute and a half retelling on the six o'clock news. Then for the ten o'clock version Jay would edit me out of the film and the anchor could do narrative over the pictures from the Phillips's house. I did not have the feeling yet that it was a major story, but I knew I had both newscasts covered for the day.

One thing I never feared was going back to the station without a story, no matter how thin I had to stretch a little bit of video and a little bit of fact. After one particular newscast Ted looked at me in astonishment. He said I had aired the most creative, inventive, and remarkable story he had ever seen in his life. He was amazed that I did a minute and a half story and said absolutely nothing. He said it should be put in a time capsule or some other secure place for posterity. His awe overcame his anger over the story's lack of substance.

"There should be some kind of award for this," he said in amazement and in front of all the other reporters and photographers. "It's a masterpiece. A masterpiece of content with no substance. Not one thing. Not one thing of substance in the story! I have never heard somebody go a minute and a half without saying a thing. You have done the impossible. You should at least take the copy and have it laminated."

Ted had quite bit of gray in his hair and many years of news experience under his belt. I was amazed that in all his years in news, I did something he had never seen or heard. I put together a flowing, logical, and creative news story that said absolutely nothing. He was flabbergasted. I was embarrassed but proud of the backhanded compliment he was giving me. I always thought I could make a story out of anything, or even, nothing. This made it official.

Because of that dubious accolade from Ted, both he and I knew I was going to get some kind of story on the air. Once we got back into town we found a pay phone to talk with the station about inside details on the story. In every media market the radio, TV stations and newspapers monitor each other to keep track of what the competition is doing, and to listen for any hint anyone else knows something on a story that they do not. With the possibility of a mass murder story ready to break, it was certain everyone had their monitors turned up and eavesdropping ears tuned in to all radio communication between the station and the news units.

Even a reporter in a news unit saying something as simple as, "I'm going ten-twenty to the courthouse," can give away a lot of information. For instance, if the reporter was Wayne from Channel Six, we knew he was one of the reporters covering the story. If he or channel 4's reporter was going to the courthouse it likely meant they were talking to someone because of a new development and we needed to make calls to catch up or at least confirm we were not missing some angle on the story.

"The sheriff's going to make a statement this afternoon," Ted told me over the phone. "If they know anything they're not letting on at this point. He'll give you the basics but he's not going to give you much else unless something big breaks on this thing in the next few hours. We're calling all around but can't get anything out of anybody. The sheriff departments and District Attorneys in Chambers and Jefferson County don't know any more about this than we do. Apparently they are absolutely clueless at this point or they have no idea where to even start looking. I've never had any contact with Sheriff Pounds and I don't know if he's got something bigger than his boys can handle dumped in his lap. Right now I know we have nothing more than a missing persons case. The only thing that bothers me about this is that there is an awful lot of his department involved in the investigation. Even as sketchy as this looks right now it doesn't take Sherlock Holmes to suspect there's a lot more to it. You don't call in the feds, the highway patrol and all the law enforcement agencies between Houston and Lake Charles unless you have something really big on your hands."

"And it doesn't take Edward R. Murrow to see I've got more suspicion than substance to try to put together a story," I answered, warning him not to expect a story of much more than the basic who, what, when and where.

I hung up the phone and turned to Jay. "Okay. Let's go to the sheriff's office. At least we'll get our talking head to put some meat into the story."

Ted and I were both right. The sheriff did not have much more to say than we already knew. No bodies, no suspects, no proof of any crime. However, from the news standpoint, the sheriff saying it made it official instead of media speculation.

My report led the 6 o'clock newscast. Standing out in front of the Phillips's house I began my story.

"In an unusual display of cooperation and coordination state and federal law officers all over Southeast Texas are trying to locate five members of the Phillips family of Winnie who disappeared over the weekend...."

With that introduction I began my first report on the disappearance of the five members of the Phillips family. Right away I knew it was a big story. Although there were few details from any law office, every reporter in the area was perking up to the specter of a real-life mystery and a story far bigger than the normal routine. You saw it in the faces of the law officers. When people saw the news logo on the side of our van or recognized me they immediately asked about the missing five.

There were several more times I stood out in the front of the house on Texas Farm to Market road 1406 using it as a prop for another report on the Phillips family. From the very first day it was obvious this was the beginning point of a strange chain of events and the house was the focal point of where it began.

What I did not know was that in the years ahead I would not only become linked to that house but also the victims, the accused, and many of the dozens of law officers and attorneys who also found their lives changed by the family and events that began inside the house.

CHAPTER THREE

Deputies Find the Car

After Monday morning the story was the focal point of every newscast. Even though Tuesday was July fourth, for the law officers and media of Southeast Texas it was not a holiday. Tuesday, Wednesday, and Thursday I was back in Winnie waiting for every little bit of utterance from Sheriff Pounds and his deputies. Any few syllables muttered by the sheriff's office gave us something fresh to add to a story that at that point was still all suspense and no substance. The fears of everyone increased every hour the family remained missing.

I was in Winnie, Ted was in the newsroom calling the Sheriff's office, district attorney, and other law enforcement agencies hourly making sure we did not miss something and trying to pry any bit of inside information out of every dispatcher, deputy, or inside-the-building flunky we could get to say something ... anything.

Like the law officers, reporters have to track down leads and dig in likely and unlikely places to find pieces to fit together into a complete picture. Often a janitor or secretary in the jail or courthouse knows what is going on behind closed doors when the law officers are not saying anything.

That is the difficult part for the reporter, finding that janitor, jailer, or deputy you have talked to before on other stories to give you some kind of insight into what's going on. Not necessarily "spill the beans for you", just mention that maybe it might be a good idea to have a camera at a certain place at a certain time or ask a certain detective a particular question about some event.

Thursday, July 6, the morning of the third day after the story broke there was nothing new. So far we rehashed the same few facts at every newscast after Monday morning. Finally that afternoon the reporters and the law officers, as well as the general public, became a lot happier with the first development in the case.

I was on the phone checking in with the newsroom when Ted gave me our game plan for the afternoon.

"They've found the car," Ted told me with relief and excitement in his voice. We finally had a new angle for the story. Every hour the story grew with suspense and intrigue. Now we had even more reason for our viewers to stay glued to every newscast for days.

"They found it down by one of the bayous in mid-county," Ted said bringing me up to speed on the story. "Totally torched. It's burned beyond all recognition. The tires, interior, wiring, everything in the trunk, burned beyond any useful evidence. All they know is that it's a car of the same body style the Phillips owned. We've got another unit going to the scene and are calling the airport to get someone to take us up for aerials. You get a statement from the Sheriff."

At this point there were a lot of smiles breaking out on the faces of reporters, photographers, editors, producers, assignment editors, copywriters, headline writers, and deputies all over Southeast Texas. It now had real intrigue. The mystery was growing about the family and concern increasing over the area that there was a crazed killer on the loose ready to abduct and kill a whole family for no reason at all.

Even before there was any new developments in the case sales of guns and ammunition increased all over the viewing area. We knew that because without new developments we were forced to do spin-off stories about the missing family. Each new bit of information was adding to the fear that it could happen again anywhere in the area. Now it was a fact. There was some kind of crime, probably a mass murder, and the murderer was still lurking out there somewhere.

At this point in a story the adrenaline begins to flow. It is not just the media. It is the sheriff's deputies, the cops in surrounding towns, and even the public in the surrounding area listening to every news broadcast for the latest information on what the police have discovered. This was a story that did not need hype. It was a real story that gripped people for hundreds of miles. Families all over Texas and into Louisiana wondered if they were in the reach of some psychopath on the loose. With each hour it became less likely the five members of the Phillips family would come walking through the door with a look of amazement on their faces and say, "What's all the commotion about? Here we are."

"During a routine patrol this afternoon a motorist flagged down Jefferson County deputy Wade Broussard. The person alerted us to a burned out car on Craigen Road alongside Taylor's Bayou," Sheriff Pounds began. "The vehicle identification number shows it belongs to Elmer Phillips of Woodward, Oklahoma, one of the five persons missing from the home of Bishop and Ester Phillips of Winnie."

"Any suspects?" the one question that had echoed from the news media for 3 days popped up again.

"We have some leads but no suspects at this time," was all that he added to the news conference.

More bantering went back and forth with questions and non-substantive answers. At that point it no longer mattered if the media got a long narrative about what was going on in the investigation.

The family was still missing; the sheriff gave us a new quote, we finally had new pictures and we had a burned out car indicating there was at least a crime of abduction.

The story that was holding the interest of every person in Southeast Texas had suddenly turned into a death grip on the consciousness of the people. It was like the times when a hurricane is wandering around in the Gulf. No one misses a newscast because everyone wants to know every development, no matter how minute. It was the topic of every conversation every time two or more people got together. That was the atmosphere that hung over Southeast Texas. People turned up their radios every time a newscast came on. People who normally did not watch the six or ten o'clock news now watched both. Newspaper racks were quickly emptying all over the area. Things like this did not happen in that corner of Texas. A crime like this was something you would expect from a big city, not Winnie. Up until this crime the only thing concerning people in Winnie was red rice. You get red rice in your field and you have problems. Mass murder was a new experience for the people of Winnie and it had their undivided attention.

For the lawmen, the media, and the general public there was now the first definitive clue that something horribly wrong had happened to the Phillips family. The worst fears were real.

Although there were few more details about what happened we got a few new facts and pictures added to the now-familiar story the media had been telling for 3 days. Even though every story started with first recounting the details about the missing family, the farm, and the odd circumstances surrounding their disappearance, there was now more fuel for speculation and more fuel for the paranoia that hung over Southeast Texas like the unrelenting heat and humidity.

The media conference went on and on with the reporters trying every angle to get the sheriff to say something he had not said before. Finally with Sheriff Pounds and the reporters exhausted from all the questions, and deadlines approaching, the sheriff politely told us he had given us all he was going to say. Jay and I started packing up our gear so we could get back to the station and get the film in the developer. It was late in the afternoon. We had our statement, we had our new film to mix in with the old, we had a new angle on the story, and less than two hours to get it on the air.

CHAPTER FOUR

A Suspect

"I want you heading straight to Winnie," Ted greeted me Friday morning. "The inside whispering is that they'll make an arrest today. Apparently they have known a lot more than they were letting on. They may have had a suspect from the very beginning."

"Any ideas about who we'll be looking for or what the person looks like," I asked trying to get a few clues to prepare me and Jay for photo opportunities.

"No," Ted responded. "It's still mostly rumor and innuendo. It may have been someone close to the family. We can't get any concrete information out of anybody. Get down to Winnie to the sheriff's office and wait for any news. Call in regularly so we can update one another and to tell us if you've moved or so we can tell you if you need to move. If anything happens before 3, let us know so we can go live."

There was a lot of speculation and rumors throughout the day but never any reason to go live. We spent the day hanging out at the sub courthouse in Port Arthur watching and waiting for the sheriff to make his move. The highlight of the day for me was spending the day with a crew from CBS out of Dallas. It was a small time reporter's high, sitting around with a network crew and listen to their recounting of stories they had covered and what it is like to leave home and travel for a month. The guys from CBS were veterans of many a stakeout and being shuttled across the country. They talked about how it is especially difficult to make a road trip for a month when they have sent you out on a 3 day assignment. There comes the problem of running out of underwear, then clean clothes. You can buy new underwear, then your suitcase starts getting full and when you get home you start running out of drawer space at home. And keeping clean clothes is a big problem too. Take them off to be cleaned or washed, and if the main office calls and sends you to another story, you may have to send back later for your spare set of clothes.

I had often thought about the glamour and prestige of being a network reporter. These were considerations about network TV I never contemplated. But on a stakeout there is plenty of time for considering things I would have never otherwise given any thought.

The dullness of the stakeout reminded me of when I was in the military stationed on Guam. I got so bored I went to the base hobby shop and made a dozen ceramic coffee mugs. I took karate lessons. I wrote letters to people I was not even sure were still alive.

When I was not contemplating life as a network reporter or remembering sitting and watching geckos run across the ceiling in my barracks on Guam, I was keeping my ears open for anything that might be happening that I did not know about. There were some good rumors circulating. There were stories whispered by other reporters that the suspect was everything from the guy next door like John Wayne Gacey to a traveling diabolical demon, or another infamous Texas mass murderer such as Henry Lucas. The images of Lucas were still familiar in the minds of Southeast Texans who watched the video of him in custody, walking over High Island with lawmen, pointing out the places to dig for the bodies of his victims.

The frustrating part is that you have to check all the rumors and take notes so that you have something just in case one of the stories is right. You have to put something on the air too. And in a worst case scenario, if the story bogs down, you at least have some speculation to share with the viewers that shows you are in there trying to dig up facts for them.

Along with the rest of the media I wound up angry, frustrated, and envious of the inside track of the *Port Arthur News* reporters. Using their connections and relentless digging, the *News* broke through the police stonewall. The **News** reporter went to the police station every day making checks and had some really good sources inside the department. All of the TV stations missed the arrest. I could not believe what happened next. A reporter from the *Port Arthur News* actually beat the police to the house of the suspect and was in the front yard talking to him when about a half dozen police and sheriff's cars drove up.

You can say the reporter scooped everyone. That is not exactly the phraseology some of the police officers used, but that is what happened. Some were pretty upset when they drove up and found a reporter asking the suspect about his impending arrest. Unfortunately for the *News* however, the arrest came late in the evening, about fourteen hours before the paper would put out another edition. So as far as the public knew, the *News'* big break on the story was ancient history by the time they could publish it.

In the middle of evening prime time all 3 stations broke into their programs announcing the Port Arthur police had arrested a suspect. The suspect taken into custody was Ovide Joe Dugas Jr. of Port Acres, a little housing development on the outskirts of Port Arthur. The public relations officer said the suspect was a worker at Texaco's main oil refinery in Port Arthur, about a mile away from the Port Acres suburb where they arrested Joe.

At last the cops had a suspect and the media had a new angle on the story. The only apprehension left was by the general public did he kill them alone? Was an accomplice still lurking out there somewhere? Someone who might strike again just for vengeance over the arrest, someone who might take hostages to try to free the suspect, someone who might kill again just to show the police he was smarter than they were? Surely there was an accomplice, still on the loose, and still in control of the situation. It was asking a little bit much of the public to believe that one person could get control over five people and then make them disappear.

At least something was happening. Now every conversation in Southeast Texas switched from speculation to, "What do you think about this guy they've arrested?" and then went directly into speculation about what had happened to that family from Winnie. For the most talked about crime of history in the area, the case was now moving relatively fast. In spite of the acceleration of the story the facts were still being devoured faster than they were becoming available. Now everyone wanted to know who this guy was. Why did he do it? How did he do it? Who helped him do it? What did he look like? Was he mean, evil, sadistic? Or even worse, was he your average looking inconspicuous guy next door type who no one would have ever suspected? The one you always read the quotes about from neighbors, "He was the nicest guy. All the kids in the neighborhood loved him."

Leading the questioning was the media that was as insatiable at this point as the rest of the public. Officially not much was coming out other than his name, address, and fact that he was a former son-in-law of Bishop and Ester Phillips, and former brother-in-law to Elmer and Martha, and former uncle to 3-year-old Jason. If this was the sheriff's suspect, the crime was beginning to shape up as a family feud more serious than anyone in Southeast Texas had ever known.

Something plainly obvious from the beginning was that the law officers were very satisfied with their work and very satisfied with their suspect. On every officer in every law organization working on the crime there was the visible look of confidence.

"They've had a suspect since Monday," Mary Dugat, a justice of the peace at the Winnie sub courthouse told me shortly before the arrest. Although I could not get any more out of her, it was something I could use for the six o'clock news. Something to throw in the story to make it sound like I was in the loop for our viewers and had an inside source that was giving me facts other than those being doled out by public relations officers for the Sheriff's department.

The arrest came down Friday evening. Dugat, the Chambers County justice of the peace who had given me the bit of inside information, issued the original arrest warrant. None of the TV stations had a photographer there. There were no photographs of this horrible person to make a still frame picture of, to show in slow motion being arrested and put in a sheriff's car with the cage inside that protects the arresting officer, and worst of all, we had a completely new chapter of the mystery and no new video to accompany the twist the investigation had taken. The only saving grace for the television stations was that the news was so anxiously awaited at that point that the information about the arrest was more important than the pictures. Pictures were good but the public wanted details.

We got all we could gather on the news, relying mainly on sound bites from official spokesmen for the Chambers County Sheriff. Since there was no new film, we spent the rest of the evening with newsbreaks blaring out the news that there was finally someone in jail awaiting charges for the abduction of the Phillips family. With the arrest of Joe and the burned car the fears of everyone greatly increased that the sheriff would soon be adding murder charges against him.

It was Friday night and there was little we could add to it at that point so I wrapped up a very long day interspersed with varying degrees of actual reporting work, boredom, and occasional excitement waiting outside courthouses, police stations, and sheriff departments by writing some more copy for the ten o'clock news to make sure we had gotten all the information available into our newscasts. Covering the story was very easy at that point. After five straight days I knew the details without having to refer to my reporter's notebook. I could not have told you how much money I had in my wallet, but I could recount the story to you down to the minutest detail. For five days it had consumed my life.

Satisfied I had done all I could to cover all the bases, I left the station and headed home, knowing I would not get beat on the arrest of a suspect, but a little concerned that something new would develop over the weekend. I was banking on the hope that just like everyone else, law officers also like quiet weekends at home with their families if there is no emergency that requires their immediate attention.

I went home feeling confident I had done all I could and feeling the glow that comes knowing everyone I would meet that weekend would want to know all the facts about the story and all the "inside" details that reporters know but can not make public because the information can not be confirmed by anyone speaking on the record.

I left with the exhilaration still flowing from the certainty that I was in the middle of the biggest murder story in history for that part of the state and that it was only going to get more exciting and interesting as the facts of the case began coming to light. It was a story that drives every reporter, the story that gives you the job satisfaction that makes up for all routine days of checking the logs at the police and fire departments and covering boring city council and county commissioner meetings. It was a compelling story and I was in the middle of it. Ask any reporter, it is exciting.

It was one of those stories that make the adrenalin flow through your veins like a drug. It is a rush that can make being a reporter an addiction. It is one of the things that sets reporting aside from other jobs. Many people put in forty or more hours a week for their entire careers and never once get a surge of excitement from doing their job. Adrenalin is the greatest legal drug there is. It is cheap. You are your own supplier. The rush feels great no matter how long it lasts or how quickly it is over. I was basking in the warmth of the moment. I was feeling that being a reporter was the best job in the world and I could never think of ever doing anything else.

Fire fighters and police officers get the same feeling. The innumerable hours of boredom and tedium on the job interspersed with the burden of paperwork suddenly seem insignificant when something happens to get their hearts pumping in overdrive. A fire chief once told me about how cranky and edgy the firemen get between fires. Along comes a blazer where they have to put their skills to use and for 3 to 4 days afterwards everybody will be in the best of moods and be the best of friends until the experience wears off.

CHAPTER FIVE

The Bodies

"They found the bodies," Ted blurted out as I walked through the newsroom door. "Without letting any of the media know they went out last night and dug them up. We didn't get anything before they left but we got some pictures earlier this morning and we're getting some more now,"

That was my "Good morning."

Once again it was Monday, there was a major break in the story and we were running to catch up with the events. Ted quickly briefed me and brought me up to speed on the latest turn in the case.

The mystery was over. There was no doubt about their fate. It was what everyone who was paying the least bit of attention had already surmised. The five of them were taken out of the house and killed. They didn't just go somewhere without telling anyone. They were not abducted and being held for ransom. There would be no ransom demands forthcoming. They were dead. It was murder. Five members of one family, including a 3-year-old, were taken out and brutally murdered. The discovery confirmed everyone's worst fears. The case was mesmerizing to law officers, reporters, and the public as well. Although it directly involved only five people, all of the area was immersed in the event, wrapped up in the fate of this quiet, country family.

The Phillips were not well known in the community. Bishop was not a Rotarian, a Lion, or a Kiwanian. Ester was not involved in a ladies' knitting club or any other women's organization. July first there probably were not a dozen people in Winnie who knew them. Now there were not a dozen people in all of Southeast Texas who did not know them, know where they lived, seen pictures of their home, been absorbed in wondering where they were, or hoped the best for them. Their disappearance had turned the entire region into an extended family wondering about the fate of relatives who could not be accounted for. It was more than a news story. It was more than a murder mystery. It was an event that touched everyone. Everyone shared in the mystery of their disappearance, the pain of losing loved ones, and the horror and repulsion of the brutal way they were killed.

"What happened?" I asked, trying to get up to speed again on the story.

"They apparently went out to the site late yesterday evening," Ted answered. "It's a spot in the woods off Highway three-sixty-five. The area is called Gilbert Woods. Apparently Joe started talking. From what I can piece together from the sheriff's department, the grave where they buried them was very well hidden and they would never have found them if someone hadn't shown them the place."

"All of them?" I asked.

"All of them. Even the baby," Ted answered.

"How were they killed?" I asked in pursuit of what was going on with the story.

"Apparently they were all shot in the head execution style. Like a professional," Ted replied.

"Gee, pretty cold-blooded," I said trying to remain objective by detaching myself from the fact that we were talking about five people. A week earlier they were gentle country people and not a news story.

"Also calculated to the last detail," Ted added. "But the story's starting to get a little frayed around the edges. I still think the cops know a lot more than they're letting on."

"Yeah, where there's this much smoke something's burning down below," I added. "What's the latest on what the sheriff office is saying?"

"Just that they've got the bodies and will be charging Dugas with murder today. Maybe we'll finally get a chance to get some pictures of him," Ted answered.

I knew what he was thinking. Some updated pictures of Joe would help obscure the fact that we were still on top of the story even though our station was not on the scene when the bodies were recovered.

"I know the place," I quickly replied. "There's a passageway behind the judge's chambers where they bring the prisoners to court. It's tight, about a yard wide, but get back in there with the camera and he has to walk right by you."

"Good," Ted smiled and said. "Get a camera and get down there."

"Don't you want a photographer back there and me in the courtroom?" I quizzed him.

"I want you both places," was his reply. "I can't give you a photographer then. You're going to have to do it yourself."

I knew that part of playing catch-up would be the photos of Joe and me standing in front of the courthouse doing a filmed intro into the story. That would put me on the scene; show the viewers we were giving them the latest details of the day to assure them that by watching our channel they were fully informed.

"What about a standup?" I asked. "You don't want me doing something this big without showing our presence down at the courthouse."

"First, get the pictures of Joe," Ted said trying to figure out the logistics of the story and the positions of other cameras and reporters covering other stories for the newscast. "Get Joe, and then if you need a standup we can have a cameraman swing by and shoot it for you. Right now I've got too many brush fires going to tie up a photographer just hanging out at the courthouse."

Because I had covered the courthouse for years and knew it inside out, I was probably the only reporter who knew, or had been in, the corridor with one end at the jail and the other in the courtroom. I had been in the passageway many times but never before to take pictures. It was a narrow passageway built into the courthouse long before there was such a thing as TV news or news cameras. The passage was designed as a secretive hallway where a prisoner could be transferred in and out of court without ever being in contact with the public or having the opportunity to attack a deputy or try to escape. It was intentionally designed to be tight quarters, basically a cement tube between lockdown and courtroom.

On my shoulder was a sixteen millimeter film camera. Mounted above the lens was a halogen light bright enough to blind you and hot enough to seriously burn you if you get too close. Around my waist was a battery belt, a leather belt approximately eight inches wide with about 15 pounds of rechargeable batteries. The belt is heavier than the weight belt a scuba diver wears. It takes a lot of battery power to illuminate an incredibly bright white light for about thirty minutes. The belt is a power pack that will give you enough electrical capacity to light up a cave but it definitely adds to your overall bulk and decreases your mobility.

It was possible that with me partially blocking what little hallway there was, my light might literally burn Joe as he walked past. I was not worried about that but I also could do the same to the officer escorting him. That was more of a problem because I did not want to do anything to upset anyone escorting Joe, such as telling the judge to ban me from the prisoner transfer passageway. And I did not want the judge mad at me even before the trial started.

Loaded like a pack mule I went into the passageway and

found me a corner in one of the many turns of its winding course to the courtroom. I was the only person in the hall. I was afraid there would be two other cameras from the other stations jamming up the hallway and the conflicting lights from all 3 cameras assuring no one got a good picture. But that did not happen. When I got in the hallway and saw know one else knew my secret, I knew I would get exclusive pictures that no other station would have.

I selected a point that would give me the maximum amount of time to get footage of him from in front, and maximum video of him from behind as he and the jailer walked past me and down the hall. Ideally I wanted him head on looking into the camera and headed for the court but there was no way I could get in front of him and walk backwards with the camera rolling. The hallway was too narrow with too many turns. I needed a lot of film because I knew every time we mentioned his name from then on; we would run the film I got in that passageway.

Poised and ready to roll, I heard sounds coming from around the corner. I was about to get my first look at the guy accused of murdering five people. I was going to get my first look at him but it would be through the eyepiece of the camera, less than a square inch view of what was happening in front of me.

I focused the camera for the point where I wanted to start rolling the film. When I heard footsteps coming towards me I aimed the camera, turned on the light and started rolling off film so that it would give the dramatic effect of him walking into my picture frame. Suddenly there he was. It was perfect. Joe was in front. I could get a long, up-close and personal view of him without the court bailiff obstructing my shot. Then for more dramatic effect, Joe would have to pass me, then the bailiff, followed by a long shot of them walking away from my camera. And best of all, I knew I had a picture of Joe that would make both the other TV stations swear in anger when they saw the photo op they had missed.

Even through the one square inch eyepiece I saw Joe was a bull of a man. He appeared to be in the maximum testosterone level of his life. He looked like he could be starting linebacker on a college team. He was very muscular and stocky looking. With his hands cuffed in front of him, he was coming towards me.

Even through my small window on the situation something looked wrong with the picture. His body looked like he had the power to rip open a tin can with his hands and teeth but in the face he looked like an average guy you would see on the street. He did not look like he had killed anyone or even thought about such things. He looked like the nice neighbor next door. But I also knew that one of the very first things a lawyer does with a grungy looking client is to cut the hair, shave the beards and mustaches and get them into a good suit before letting them go out in public.

As he came to the ninety degree angle in the hallway where I was pressed as far back in the corner as I could get, instead of complaining to the bailiff, shoving me, giving me a dirty look, or giving me some choice comments on his thoughts about me being there, he meekly ducked and twisted, almost apologetically, as best he could to get by me without interfering with me getting my pictures. The corridor was intentionally designed so confining to keep a reluctant prisoner from getting any ideas about thinking he could overpower a bailiff and escape. We had such a narrow space to share that he brushed my left arm and slightly jarred the picture for a few frames. The jailer angled himself so that Joe was blocking his face from the camera. When I turned the camera to film Joe walking away, then the deputy from the jail stepped in front of me when I could only get a picture of him from behind.

As they walked away from me I was thinking the guy I saw through my viewfinder did not seem like such a bad guy. It was not until about a month later that fear hit me when testimony began in the courtroom and I heard the sadistic things he had done to his former wife and kids. My ineptitude at judging character scared me too. When I heard in testimony from his former wife, brothers, and others who knew about some of the things he had done, I realized for the first time that I had been extremely vulnerable in that hallway the day I first saw and took pictures of him. Even with handcuffs on him he could have seriously hurt me before the jailer restrained him. Looking through the camera lens directly into his face, both my hands supporting the camera, I would have never seen what was coming if he had wanted to express his feelings about me and the camera at that moment. I was shocked at how relaxed and comfortable I had been with him where we literally brushed up against one another in a situation that gave him plenty of reason to explode in anger. As I heard when the first details about his personality started leaking from inside sources, anger and a hair-trigger temper were definitely two of his more predominant personality traits.

Through the camera lens I had one picture of him as a submissive young man going obediently to court as requested. In the courtroom as the case unfolded I got another picture. It was the picture of a belligerent bully lurking beneath the guy-next-door image. It was the picture of an inner rage that made me cringe to think of what violence and destruction could be unleashed in that muscular body.

CHAPTER SIX

Joe Talks

"We need you at the courthouse at ten," Ted briefed me on my assignment for the day. "Apparently the DA has another suspect and they're getting ready to go public. I want you to take production's video camera. We won't have time to develop film and we've got to have this on the noon news."

"Great," I answered. "Have you been able to get anything out of them?"

"It's a woman. A housewife from Nederland," Ted filled me in. "They're not giving out a lot of information. But they seem pretty confident about what they're saying."

"A housewife," I asked? "What is this, some kind of Bonnie and Clyde thing? Or a Betty Crocker and Clyde thing?"

"May be," Ted replied. "Or maybe an amateurish attempt at Bonnie and Clyde. Get on down to the courthouse and keep us updated so we can make sure we've got the full story by noon. Get what video you can and put together a full package for the six and ten newscasts."

When I got to the courthouse there were all the print, radio, and TV reporters from the Beaumont area, plus ones from Houston and Lake Charles, Louisiana. Five people dead, including a baby and the District Attorney was saying a housewife was involved. Could it really be that the heinous accomplice that was there and a part of this brutal mass murder had been watching the arrest of Joe, the finding of the bodies, all the while hiding behind a white picket fence, a house in the suburbs, hiding in the kitchen behind an apron? This was our monster? A housewife with cookie dough on her hands?

The Phillips' home was just outside of Winnie in Chambers County. The grave where the five were buried was about seventeen miles north of that and just a mile or two into Jefferson County. All the various law departments involved agreed that the abduction happened in Chambers County, but Elmer Phillips's car was found in Jefferson County and the murders apparently took place at the grave site in that county as well. They also agreed Chambers County was not suited for all the media attention the trials would draw, and the Jefferson County District Attorney's office had a much larger staff and was better prepared and more eager to take on a case of this magnitude. So by mutual agreement Jefferson County became the setting for the trial. Of course this elated me and every reporter in the Beaumont-Port Arthur area as it put the trial on our home turf.

James McGrath, the District Attorney for Jefferson County, came into the room and sat down positioning himself behind the microphones and allowing all the photographers to get a focus on him while reporters opened notebooks and pushed buttons on tape recorders. He was visibly anxious to give the public the details of the case and not the least bit intimidated by all the reporters, note pads, tape recorders and bright lights of all the TV cameras. He knew everyone in Southeast Texas would be hanging on every word he spoke and quoting him over and over again the following day.

McGrath was in his 50's, short and stocky. He wore dark framed glasses and still had a few strands of hair left that he put into place with his right hand as he waited for everyone to get into position for his statement. On his face he had the look of a bulldog that had come from more than twenty years as both a defense and a prosecuting attorney. Although he had defended many criminal clients it was clear that he relished his roll of district attorney and delighted in putting bad guys behind bars. He relished center stage, whether in front of TV cameras or in the drama of the courtroom.

"Through the combined efforts of the entire law enforcement community of Southeast Texas, we have gathered the evidence to make charges against an additional suspect in connection with the abduction and murders of the Bishop Phillips family of Winnie," McGrath spoke into the glare of camera lights with confidence and the appearance that he wanted the trial to start that day. "Linda May Burnett of Nederland will be arraigned this afternoon and charged with capital murder as an accomplice to Joe Dugas, the suspect we already have in custody."

"Will there be any other arrests?" a question came in from behind the camera lights.

"No," again McGrath answered without hesitation. "At this time we have no reason to suspect any other participants in the case. However, the investigation is still on going."

"Who is she, what links her to the crime?" came another question from the mob of reporters along with all the assistant district attorneys, and curious secretaries and lawyers in the room.

McGrath curled his lower lip and went on the attack again. "She is a housewife from Nederland. She is a friend of Joe Dugas and witnesses saw her with him during the time frame of when we believe the murders took place."

"Does she have a criminal record?" I jumped in to get my voice on a question and place our station's presence at the news conference.

McGrath turned his head and looked directly at me, with his best somber and emotionless news-conference-face. "No. This is the first time she's ever been accused of committing a crime."

"What makes you think a first timer would commit such a big league crime?" I quickly followed up with a rather obvious question.

"I won't go into the specifics of the case now," McGrath continued, "but we have what we believe to be sufficient evidence and witnesses' testimony to suspect that she was a partner in the commission of the crime."

After the news conference I was one of the reporters and photographers descending on the second floor of the courthouse as the time drew near for Linda's arraignment. Suddenly everyone in the hallway and offices stopped what they were doing to get a look at her. The only movement was photographers jockeying for position for the first look at our home-grown mass murderer. She was a short, frail looking woman, appearing to weigh less than 100 pounds. *This was the fiendish monster that had been lurking out there eluding the cops, deputies, and FBI agents from Houston to Baton Rouge? This was our monster baby-killer?"* Everyone stood staring. No one spoke above a whisper. Even people on the floor for other courts stopped to take their concentration off their legal problems and focused on her.

Linda went into the District Clerk's office with her counsel and went back to the coffee area to sit down while she waited for the next word from the court as to what papers and motions were to be filed and what her options were at that point. It was during this time that something unexpected happened. Several of the other reporters were standing, whispering, and pointing in her direction as if she were some alien from another planet to be observed from a distance until it could be determined whether she was malevolent or benign. Then I realized what was wrong with the scene. She was all alone in the coffee area. There she was, without her attorney or any law officer. A smile came to my face. It was a golden opportunity, a reporter's dream come true, total access to an accused mass murderer.

I had interviewed movie stars, music stars, political stars, and sports stars. I have high school and college friends who have served time. A college friend of mine went on to become Dallas' "Friendly Rapist" so Linda's notoriety did not impress or intimidate me. Knowing an opportunity like this probably would not come up again; I figured "what the heck." I walked over and sat down beside her. She appeared slightly older than 31 years. She looked at me and smiled.

I may have said, "Hi." I'm not certain. I do know that whatever I said, I did not get a chance to say much more. With no hesitation whatsoever she started talking as fast as I have ever heard anyone talk and I quickly learned from her that her nickname was "motormouth" as she apologized for talking so much. I learned many other things about her as well but she was rattling everything off quicker than I could write down or ingest. Even if I had known shorthand I do not think I could have kept pace with her. She talked about having seen me on TV many times, what news she watched, what papers she read, and a continuing list of other topics that ran on longer than I had room for in my note pad even if I could have kept up with her. The conversation seemed so fast that it is just a blur in my memory. She talked about her young daughters, her husband and how she loved living in Nederland. She mentioned that when she had worked at a donut shop there in Nederland she had met some of the lawmen who were now building their case and preparing to testify against her in court. She talked about what nice men they were and how she knew it was nothing personal, they were just doing their jobs. She followed that up by saying she held no grudge against them because she knew this was all just a big mistake and she would soon be back home with her husband and kids. I sat there listening, my mind spinning and thinking one of us was in total denial.

She was charming, immediately captivating, and appeared to be nothing more than any housewife you would find in any home in any small American town. She was open and willing to talk at length about anything before her arrest. In less than ten minutes she poured out her entire life history, up to her arrest. She never ran out of words or things to talk about. I sat there amazed. Two sentences together without a script is a strain for my meager conversational skills. And my mind was telling me, *"Don't screw this up. Keep your mouth shut. Let her talk!"*

All her friends and family called her Linda. But after her arrest and McGrath spoke her full name, Linda May Burnett, from that moment on she became Linda May. All you had to do was say Linda May and every person in a two hundred mile radius immediately had a mental picture of the frail little woman seen in all the TV news reports and newspaper photos.

While we talked, others stared. Now the whispering had gone from "there she is, it's her. Linda May!" to, "I can't believe he's talking to her!" and "I can't believe her lawyer hasn't swooped in and stopped her from talking to him. He's a reporter!" In the middle of all the amazement I was the most astounded. I was sitting next to a person accused of committing mass murder and talking as if we were discussing last Sunday's picnic after church. As she talked my mind whirled with the thought of what odd situations being a reporter can get you into and what a variety of famous, infamous, dull, funny, downright angry, and interesting people you meet while doing your job. She was certainly one of the most fascinating persons I had ever met.

While she talked I thought, "*How could this woman have any secrets?*" Surely if she was questioned by the sheriff's office it would have been like turning on a spigot. You did not have to be an experienced interrogator to get information out of her. The only problem was keeping up with all the information that flowed so freely from her. And then I thought, *what difference does it make? This is Texas. Justice comes at the end of a rope.*

We talked for several minutes before her attorney appeared and motioned for her to come over to him. Since she did all the talking the topic of the circumstances that brought her to the courthouse never came up. She did say she had to be careful about what she said because her attorney had warned her about talking too much. Glancing up and acknowledging her attorney beckoning, she said she was sorry but she had to go. She got up and went out in the hall with her attorney where they began discussing the legal maneuvering going on. At that point she was still free on bond and could come and go from the courthouse as she pleased.

After she left I was a little disappointed she did not "commit news" by saying something quotable about the case but I was more taken by what an interesting experience it had been to talk to her. I was right about taking advantage of the situation; it was the last time while she was free on bond that her lawyers allowed her to stray through the courthouse by herself.

She remembered that small act of kindness towards her and through the many days and dozens of court appearances she would always look for me when entering the courtroom and always say "hi," or wave to acknowledge my presence. Naturally, this made me the butt of a lot of jokes and seriously crude accusations from other reporters. Even the judge and district attorney ribbed me about it on a regular basis. There were many times when the trial got boring or during breaks that someone would bring out a Roger & Linda joke. It always got a laugh and broke the tedium of the trial.

For years we corresponded and she replied in long, handwritten letters. One Christmas she knitted little angels for me, my wife and daughters to hang on our Christmas tree. Every year they are brought out of the decorations box and hung on the tree.

CHAPTER SEVEN

The Trial

"We're going to try Linda May first," McGrath stoically announced into the glare of TV lights and mass of wires, recorders, microphones and reporters assembled for his news conference.

"Why her, why not Joe?" came the question from a reporter.

It did seem more logical, and in Texas reasoning, more manly to go for the big trophy first. *Why pick on this dainty little woman when there's a really big, bad guy, a bully standing away from the spotlight watching from the security and comfort of his county supplied room and board?* Five people murdered. That's a man's handiwork. It was not the kind of work you would associate with a ninety-eight pound woman. I wanted to see the really bad guy locked away. Not a little woman.

"We think her trial will be the easier of the two to put on and we think the citizens of Jefferson County have a right to form the jury for her and hear first hand of what happened down there at that farm house on the outskirts of Winnie," McGrath answered the reporter. "And there's less chance for a change of venue in her case."

"You'll try her for all five of the murders?" a question

quickly came from another reporter.

"No," McGrath fired back. "We'll be trying her for the murder of the uh, little baby, uh, Jason."

Puzzled with this legal logic I asked, "Why the baby? Why not all five?"

I loved watching McGrath when he was on the attack and I knew he loved center stage. He curled his lower lip, and then gave a very self-assured answer. "For two reasons. First, we believe it will be easier to get a conviction on the baby. Second, if we don't get a conviction, we can come back and try her again for the murder of one of the others."

"And what if you don't get a conviction then?" another reporter chimed in.

"Then we'll try her again," McGrath said as if he had anticipated the question for weeks. "We'll go right down the line and try her five times for the murder of each one if that's what it takes to get a conviction. We're prepared to do that, yes."

"But," McGrath quickly interjected, "We don't think that will happen. We're very certain we'll get a conviction the first time. I don't see us having to try her more than once. Once all the facts are known."

"Will you go for the death sentence if you get a conviction?" another reporter asked.

Keeping his stone face, McGrath abruptly answered, "Yes. Most definitely."

"Which court will you try the case in? Gist or Giblin?" a radio reporter asked.

"If we are successful in preventing a change of venue," McGrath turned and looked at the reporter, "we will try it here in Judge Larry Gist's Criminal District Court."

Long before this case I sat in McGrath's office, interviewing him on and off camera. We even talked about his war experiences in New Guinea. Cut off from supplies and reinforcements, he and a few others had to survive on nothing but cashew nuts for almost a month. We also talked about how he loved guns. Later I took my rare, four shot derringer into his office to let him look at it and give his appraisal. I winced when he pulled back the trigger and dry fired it. I thought if he really knew guns he knew you do not dry-fire them.

Professionally and privately I knew McGrath wanted this trial. This was a crime of legendary proportions. Putting away a mass murderer was good politics. He had only been in office for two months. This trial could assure him of many more election victories. Through the thousands of news stories that would be generated by this trial his name would appear in every media dozens of times a day. It would forever burn his name into the minds of the voters of Southeast Texas. More than that, this was the most sensational trial ever in that stretch of land along the Gulf coast and it touched an emotional raw nerve with the public, the media, law offices, and McGrath, a relentless prosecutor.

He was at the height of his law career, the height of his mental acumen, and the height of his vengeance in wanting to put these two away. I knew it was more than another day at the office for McGrath. He made it obvious to everyone that he wanted justice done and he wanted to be the prosecutor who sent Joe and Linda to the death chamber. For McGrath this was a little bit law, and a whole lot of vengeance. He was emotionally involved and personally repulsed by the heinousness of this crime. Talking with him one-on-one in his office or in the news conferences it was plain to see he was inflamed with passion for this case. And he knew a prosecutor in Texas would be much more electable with a couple of convictions for capital punishments on his resume. Re-election was also a highly motivating issue for McGrath. He was appointed to the District Attorney's office when the previous DA left to take another appointed position. McGrath liked the office, the title, the job and wanted to stay in the position for a long time. This trial could guarantee all of the above.

Even with all the suspense, the arrests, and other hype

leading up to this point, McGrath's enthusiasm for the trial was spreading to me and the rest of the reporters. He was practically salivating to try both Joe and Linda and it was easy to see why after he began to let out a few of the details. The deck was stacked in his favor. Joe had started talking to his brother and the perfect crime began unraveling before anyone knew the five were missing from their farm house. It was the perfect crime. There is only one problem with committing the perfect crime. How do you take credit for the perfect crime without claiming it as yours? The officers who went to the grave site with Joe said the grave was perfectly camouflaged. They said if he had not pointed the grave out to them they could have walked over it hundreds of times without ever realizing where the bodies lay. It even took Joe a few attempts to find the grave.

In the hall one day McGrath told me off the record, "If Joe hadn't started talking; the Phillips's disappearance would have been an unsolved mystery in Southeast Texas until maybe a hundred years from now, a housing development might be built in Gilbert Woods and their bones unearthed. It was a perfectly planned and executed crime. Everything went their way. There wasn't one uncontrollable event to upset their plan. No one drove by the house on Winnie and saw them. The road in front of the Phillips house went straight north for about five miles where it was intersected by Highway three-sixty-five. Both are back roads with little traffic. At the intersection of the two roads the two cars turned right down three-sixty-five and drove about eight or nine miles to a lonely spot in the road where the grave was waiting about twenty feet into the woods. No one saw them driving north on farm to market fourteen-O-six. No one drove down three-sixty-five and saw them at the grave site. No one heard the gunshots. Not one fingerprint at the Phillips's house. Nothing. Not a microscopic bit of evidence to link either Joe or Linda to the crime."

McGrath also wanted to try the case with the home field advantage. He wanted all the gory details laid out in front of the voters in Southeast Texas who elect a district attorney every four years.

The defense wanted the trial anywhere but Jefferson County, hopefully El Paso, 890 miles away. It is as far away from Beaumont as you can get and still be in Texas so one of the first motions filed by the defense was for a change of venue. The hearing was scheduled and members of every news media in the area were subpoenaed to testify about the extent of the coverage the case had generated.

"We've got the tapes and transcripts of everything we've broadcast," Ted assured me. "You've done most of the reporting on the story so you can testify about all the stories we've aired. There's no need for me to go down there."

This would be interesting. I had sat through hundreds of hours of courtroom testimony and saw witnesses turn to stone, turn to putty, break down, become defiant, quiver, cry, and lie; but mostly just try as honestly as possible to tell the truth. For the first time I was going to find out what it is like to have a microphone about a foot in front of my face capturing everything I say while watching a court recorder a few feet away transcribing it for the record. It was not me on trial but it is still unnerving to know anything you say can be held against you. Especially when the rest of the media sat in the courtroom smirking while they waited for those little beads of sweat to start popping out on my upper lip.

As he would through most of the trial, First Assistant District Attorney Gerald Flatten handled most of the questioning for the State. He was very thin with just a hint of his blond hair visible on the sides of his head. He always wore a shirt about two inches bigger than his neck so that there was at least an inch gap between his neck and collar. I knew Flatten and he is one of the funniest and most enjoyable persons to be around but in court he is strictly professional and without a trace of emotion.

"Mr. Daniel, how long have you worked for your current employer?"

"About two and a half years," I began with only a slight crack in my voice as my nerves gave me a case of cotton mouth.

Flatten then asked some standard questions affirming I was who I said I was and worked for who I said. The questions were logical but laughable because I knew everyone in the courtroom, including the judge, on a first name basis and had been working with them since my first week as a reporter in Southeast Texas. I had laughed and joked with every attorney in the room, the bailiffs, court recorder, and secretaries down the hall and more than once been in Judge Gist's chamber for a drink with him and several lawyers so preliminary questions were a formality, but a necessary one for the record.

"As a reporter for that station," Flatten asked while fiddling with a pencil between his fingers and distracting me, "do you have knowledge of the extent of your station's coverage of the murder of the Bishop Phillips family in Winnie?"

"Yes I do," I replied, thinking, *please don't ask me anything tough or that will show me up in front of the other media.*

Flatten cocked his head slightly to the left and asked, "How would you describe the extent of the coverage your station has given this story?"

"All I can say with certainty is that in the two and a half years I've been employed there," I answered, "the station has never devoted more manpower, film and video, and air time to any other story."

"Thank you Mr. Daniel." Flatten turned to the judge. "We have no further questions your honor. We pass the witness."

Judge Gist turned his head to his right and looked down from the bench at Linda's attorneys. "No questions your honor. We pass the witness."

Judge Gist turned to his left and asked the State, "Any further questions?"

"No your honor."

"Witness excused. Call your next witness."

That was it? That was my big grilling on the witness stand. What was the State trying to do? Give up without a fight? I was a little disappointed. But mostly relieved. I did not get caught in a lie, even though there was nothing to lie about. Neither the State nor defense embarrassed me by asking how many viewers watched our news. I would have gone on record saying we had the smallest TV audience share of the 3 stations in the area. I was happy that I did not look amateurish in front of the other media. And my fly was not open. That was the biggest relief of all. It was an odd and unnerving experience. I was not accused of anything. I was not on trial. But no matter what the circumstances I never want to testify in court again.

Some of the other radio stations gave testimony and a whole lot of stories and audio and video tapes submitted as evidence. Despite all the pretrial publicity Judge Gist denied the request and ordered the trial held in Jefferson County. A small victory for the State legally speaking but a big victory for McGrath in securing the home field advantage throughout the trial. McGrath wanted to try Linda first and he wanted to try her in his arena. He could not have cared less about Dugas. He was confident he could easily get a conviction against Joe anywhere in the state of Texas, or any other state of the defense's choice. He knew once he laid out the facts about Joe, a jury anywhere, anytime, would convict him of anything, just to get him off the streets.

The decision for a Jefferson County trial was a relief to me as well. I knew if the trial was moved to El Paso, 890 miles away, my station would work out some kind of trade-off with an El Paso station to cover the trial. Our station was number 3 in the market for a good reason. We did not have the money, manpower or motivation to invest that kind of expense into a trial.

With that pretrial motion out of the way, Judge Gist set a court date for jury selection. It was a month long process. The State decided they would pursue capital murder charges. If they got a conviction Linda would become the only woman on death row in Texas. So one of the questions asked every prospective juror dealt with their ability to sentence someone to death. Although jury selection is pretty dull and tedious with the same questions asked over and over, there were a few moments of tension and levity that never made it into the court record. I do not know if it was her allergies from years of living next door to major oil refineries in Nederland, or because she would sometimes cry a bit as allegations were made against her, but Linda always had a wadded up tissue in her hand that she used to wipe her nose. One day she became very upset with something Flatten was saying about her and she threw her used, wadded up tissue at him. Although just a tissue, it had been used enough to give it some weight and fly across her defendant's table toward Flatten, about 10 feet away. Her aim was off and it bounced harmlessly off the State's table and on to the floor. Flatten later joked that fortunately it had not been used enough to actually be a biological weapon.

After many questions, potential jurors and used tissues, a jury was selected of eight men and four women. Eight of the jurors were refinery workers. Three of them worked in the same Texaco processing plant in Port Arthur where Linda's codefendant Dugas worked.

When the day finally arrived and the judge's gavel came down calling the court to order, the strategies of the State and defense began to come into focus.

A common technique defense lawyers use in a trial is to put everyone on trial except their client. Put the spotlight somewhere else so it only casts a shadow of a doubt on the defendant. Blame an accomplice, blame an acquaintance, blame it on insanity, blame it on the weather, just do not blame it on my client.

In this trial Linda was the defendant but it seemed as if even the State was putting Joe on trial. Joe's name came up again and again but Linda's was rarely mentioned. Throughout pretrial motions and hearings and Linda's trial, the main focus of the State's case was directed at Joe Dugas. Assistant District Attorney Flatten would usually begin the questioning.

Flatten had just recently taken the job as the first assistant district attorney. He had been a successful attorney in Houston when McGrath hired him. Flatten looked the lawyer part. He always wore expensive looking suits with a white shirt. The shirts had about an inch gap between his shirt and neck as if he had an irrational fear of being in tight places.

When Flatten was not focused on a case he had an engaging sense of humor. Once when challenged about the authenticity of a particular word he bet the other person there was no such word in the dictionary. Taking the bet the other person got a dictionary and pointed the word out to Flatten. Instead of admitting defeat, he grabbed the corner of the page, ripped the page out of the dictionary. As he did he laughed and said, "See, I told you there's no such word in the dictionary."

There was no joking now. Flatten focused on the people on trial and the case the cops and district attorney's office had assembled. The State was ready. The defense was ready. The large, 1930 era Criminal District Court was packed to capacity as almost 200 court groupies, curiosity seekers, courthouse workers, and reporters were packed inside, ready for the biggest trial, the biggest media spectacle, and the biggest event in the court's history began. The 132nd District courtroom was the largest in the county and built for trials like this, large, to accommodate as many of the public as possible to hear trials of great importance to the community. It was well lit on two sides with huge windows. All the furniture inside was a dark, luxurious looking wood. The courthouse was built long before air conditioning and the ceilings were two stories high, to cool it in the summer time and give it the appearance of a massive arena where noble men meet to debate heavy matters of criminal accusations. It had the aura of grandeur that made the presiding judge appear to have an even greater amount of judicial clout. If you were the defendant, it was very intimidating.

The room was huge. The ceiling I estimated was 50 or more feet. The wood was all dark, apparently to give it a somber feeling that all matters considered in it were thoughtfully and thoroughly weighed by the most legally astute minds. It was built during the short lived reign of art deco. Sitting in it was like looking through a window into the past. It was too big, too ornate, and too expensive to belong to the modern era. The courthouse was built when the philosophy was that it was a public trial and the public, as many of them as wanted to hear what was going on, should be given the opportunity to come in, sit down, and listen to the justice system at work, and in Texas terms, "give 'em a fair trial and hang 'em."

When he put on his black robe Judge Gist was the perfect picture of a judge. He had a thick head of salt and pepper hair, and a thick salt and pepper beard. Prior to the trial I saw some historical photos of Jefferson County lawyers, including a young Gist without a beard. Judge Gist had no chin. With the thick, luxurious beard cut to a point where most people have a chin, the beard gave him the illusion of having a jutting chin, and a much more judicial look about him. The beard served him well.

Richard Dugas, Joe's brother, was the first witness called. He nervously and awkwardly sat down in the witness chair and avoided eye contact with everyone in the courtroom as the bailiff adjusted the microphone in front of him. Richard was dressed nicely, but everything he wore was off the rack and gave him an air of just plain country folk.

Flatten began the State's case. "When was the first time you saw your brother Joe after the disappearance of the Phillips family?"

"It was Monday afternoon, July third, at my house,"

"What did Joe say was the purpose of his visit that afternoon?"

"He gave me forty dollars."

"Did he say why he was giving you forty dollars?"

"He said it was for the twenty-two rifle he borrowed from me. He said he'd taken care of some business and he disposed of the rifle. He couldn't bring the rifle back so he was paying me for it."

"Before he brought you this forty dollars had he ever

mentioned killing his in-laws?"

"Yes," Richard nervously answered.

"Why did he bring this up to you?"

"He wanted me to help him kill them."

"How many times had he asked you to help him kill them?"

"Two or three times."

Flatten shifted the questioning away from that encounter. "When was the next time you saw your brother Joe?"

Richard tensely squirmed in his chair as if he could somehow dodge the question. "The next day."

"And the next day, what did he tell you?"

Richard put his head down and nervously mumbled, "He said, 'I think I've committed the perfect crime.'"

"Excuse me, could you lean forward and repeat your answer directly into the microphone?"

"He said, 'I think I've committed the perfect crime.'"

"Did he tell you anything else about this perfect crime?"

"He told me the whole story," Richard responded with his eyes lowered to the railing in front of him. The words came with more difficulty as he continued recounting the second meeting with Joe. "He told me the whole story from beginning to end. He even showed me a blister on his hand that he got from digging the grave."

Richard had already given this account to the Vidor police department July 7. Vidor is in Orange County, the first county you enter when you come from Louisiana into Texas on Interstate 10. When Richard talked to the Vidor police he officially tied every law enforcement jurisdiction in Southeast Texas to the case. Acting on the information Richard gave them; investigators went to Joe's house and took evidence from it, including a K-Bar knife and a Gold Cup forty-five pistol.

"He said he took his car to the Rodair Club as an alibi. He and the woman with him dressed in jungle fatigues. He said they went out to the house and he cut the screen to get in. He said he and the woman were armed. They used the kid to control the adults. He said they told them to cooperate or they'd hurt the kid. He told how he handcuffed the old man, tied up the women and used the little boy to control them. He said everything had gone fine, not one flaw from the beginning until the end."

"Did he say there was any skirmish with them at the house?"

"Joe said he pistol-whipped the old man with the butt of his forty-five and the old man was bleeding all over the place. He said they had to get a pillow case and wipe up all the blood."

"Did he tell you who killed the five of them?"

"He said she killed the four adults but she refused to kill the baby." The words came very slow and torturous from Richard. "He said she forced him to kill the kid."

"Did he tell you the name of this woman who shot the four adults?"

"No."

"Did he give you any reason why he wouldn't name her?"

"Me and my brother Roy were in the car with him. He said he didn't want to use any names because he didn't want to get us in trouble."

"Did he say what was used to kill them?"

"Yes. My twenty-two."

"And at that time did he tell you what he had done with your twenty-two?"

"He said he'd taken it apart and thrown all of the parts away."

"This was on Tuesday, July the Fourth, six days before there was anything in the media that the Phillips family had been murdered and buried in a grave off of Highway three-sixty-five?"

"That's right, before anyone knew what had happened to them."

"You've testified Joe asked you to help him kill his in-laws. Back then, did you think he was serious?"

I could see from the anguish on Richard's face that he clearly did not want to answer the questions but something, his honesty, or possibly threats from the DA to be tried as an accessory, made him testify.

"No. Joe had a big mouth."

"Has he ever threatened you or any of your family?"

Richard's discomfort continued, but his voice strengthened as he told about Joe's past. "He's threatened to kill Mom many times. When we went to see him in jail in Winnie he got mad and said, 'I'm going to kill you sons of bitches. All of you!'"

"Had he ever threatened to kill anyone outside of your family or the Phillips family?"

"He had gotten into fistfights and gunfights with several people."

"Were you afraid of him?" Flatten asked getting more personal.

Richard again squirmed in his chair as the question came out. He never let his eyes drift away from Flatten.

"I knew he was an expert marksman and I knew he had seven or eight guns. But I didn't think he could kill five people."

"Richard," Flatten continued as he looked down at his legal pad, "this is quite a story to be telling about your own brother. Why would you tell this to anyone?"

Not once since taking the witness stand had Richard let his eyes stray from the railing in front of him or Flatten when he spoke. "Because I had a moral obligation," he answered on the verge of choking up. "He blamed all his troubles on his in-laws. He said all his problems with his wife were because of the old man and woman. I couldn't let anyone go around killing people because of some … he paused as he strained through his emotions to almost yell out … "because of some dumb grudge."

With that dramatic outburst Flatten paused, turned to Judge Gist, and with a deadpanned look, said, "We pass the witness."

Judge Gist turned to Linda's attorneys. "Any questions?"

"No your honor."

"State can call the next witness."

Richard was excused and with great sorrow and pain in his face he stepped down from the witness stand as the bailiff went to the hallway to call Mary Dugas, Joe's former wife, to testify. Mary came into the courtroom. She was a stout woman, wearing a plain dress with a straight, short hairstyle. It seemed to me that she had been through a tough life and appeared older than she was. She wore no makeup and looked as if she never did anything in the way of trying to improve her appearance. Without ever letting her eyesight dart in the direction of Linda or the State, Mary began recounting what it was like to live a life in the day of Joe Dugas. She told the court that after she left Joe he made threats almost daily in an attempt to force her and the children to come back to him. She testified Bishop and Ester never got along with Joe and they knew of his brutal treatment of their daughter. She talked about the many fights between Joe and the old couple. They knew he was mean and dangerous. They also knew he had an arsenal of guns and knives and not only would use them, but use them with skill. Bishop and Ester feared for the safety of their daughter, their grandchildren, and themselves. They never knew what Joe would do when he got angry. She and Joe were married for seven years before they divorced. After the divorce Joe moved back into the house until "he got back on his feet."

The State's plan was to use Mary to paint a picture of Joe as a mean, revenge-bent trouble maker who could become violent at the slightest provocation. The plan worked immediately. "I was scared to death of him," she answered when asked why she let him stay in her house after their divorce. She testified Joe told her he would never leave nor would he allow her to go. He stayed there until it finally got too much for her and their kids to take any longer. When the threat of being murdered became less than the pain of staying with him she moved out. She told the court she finally moved out two months before the murder of her five relatives.

Flatten continued questioning her. "When Joe got angry and violent, what would he do?"

Without emotion, she answered, "His violence was almost always with a gun or a knife."

"Was there any particular thing that made him angry and get a gun or a knife? Was there a reason he would have these violent outbursts?"

"No. He would get angry over anything that didn't please him."

"After he got a gun, did he ever shoot at you?"

"Yes."

"Could you tell us about the most recent incident of Joe shooting at you?"

"It was one night earlier in the year," Mary answered in a monotone, as if numbed by the repeated acts of violence against her and the children. "He took me out to a pasture. He had a gun and he shot at me."

"Was he trying to kill you?"

"I could hear the bullets whizzing by. I think he just wanted to scare me because it wasn't the first time he'd shot at me and he'd had plenty of opportunity to hit me," she replied. She knew Joe was an excellent marksman with pistols and rifles and could easily hit a motionless, terrified target from a short distance away.

"And did he say why he was shooting at you?"

"He told me he thought I was screwing around with his brother."

"Did he ever use anything other than a gun to frighten or intimidate you?"

"He held a knife on me too many times to count. He tied me to the bed. He held a gun to my head. This went on all through our marriage," Mary droned on. "There were acts of violence on me or the kids at least once or twice a week the whole time we were married. He shot at me at least ten times. It's just one big blur."

I could not understand it. Not only Mary, but her children as well had been put through a personal hell living with Joe. How could she sit there on the witness stand and recount a daily schedule of horrendous events like she was reading something as mundane as a grocery list?

"Were there other incidents where you were threatened?"

"Once he took my curling iron and burned my butt," she answered as if detaching herself from human emotions was the only way to remember the incident. "He threatened to ram it up my vagina."

The atmosphere in the courtroom noticeably shifted. The testimony up until that point was dramatic but not so sadistic in such a personal way. On the row where I sat with the rest of the reporters I saw everyone's pens flying across their notepads.

"Did you think he would carry through on the threat?"

"With Joe you had to take every threat seriously."

"What brought on this particular incident?"

"The same as the others. He was always accusing me of fooling around on him."

Flatten changed course to go into other times Joe showed his sadistic side. "Was there ever a threat you considered more serious that Joe made against you?"

"Yes, once he took a blowtorch to me."

"Did he tell you his reason for doing that?"

"He was accusing me of fooling around on him again."

"And what did he say he was going to do with the blowtorch?"

"He said he was going to seal my vagina shut," she said with a blank face, looking as if Joe had sapped out of her all her ability to feel.

Until then the only sound in the courtroom was Flatten and Mary. No one coughed. No one unwrapped a stick of gum or piece of candy. Everyone was motionless in fear that if they made the slightest sound they would miss her riveting testimony. But this statement brought audible moans and gasps. My face contorted in disgust at her answer. I tried my best to keep up, but with those words I put down my pen and raised my eyes to the witness stand. I could not believe what I was hearing. I heard muffled crying coming from the defense table and looked over to see the crying came from Linda. I did not know why she was crying. Was it sympathy? Was it empathy? Or was it because she was sensing her chances of ever being free again disappear with every word Mary spoke?

"How serious was Joe? Did he follow through with this threat?"

Mary's facial expression never changed. Her voice never changed. Like a robot, with her eyes devoid of life, she continued her story. "He had me on the floor on my stomach. He got close enough to me that I could feel the heat from the blowtorch."

Reporters and people in the courtroom squirmed in their seats and had looks of nausea on their faces from this sickening testimony. Linda cried silently between her attorneys as she listened to Mary go through what seemed an unending list of Joe's acts of brutality.

From pretrial debriefings Flatten knew exactly how she was going to reply to his next question. "Did he ever threaten to kill you and dispose of your body?"

"He threatened to kill me and the kids many times. Just before I left him in May, he said, 'I'll use a rubber hose. I'll kill your ass and I'll hide your body where no one will ever find it.'"

I cringed as she recounted the brutal acts of violence against her and the kids. I felt sorry that any person should have to live with such brutality. As I thought about what he did to her, for the first time terror hit me when I realized that before the trial I was so close to him that he brushed up against me in that narrow prisoner transfer corridor. Even if he was a coward when the odds were not heavily in his favor, he was genuinely evil and at that moment I was totally vulnerable.

CHAPTER EIGHT

Linda's Defense Team

After her arrest Linda hired Joe Goodwin to represent her. Goodwin was getting elderly and having health problems but was still a very powerful and well respected attorney. Before the trial I went to his office to interview him. I remember feeling like a part of history when I looked on the wall and saw a picture of him with Jack Ruby. He was Ruby's attorney after Ruby shot and killed Lee Harvey Oswald in front of millions of us watching on TV. From his defense of Ruby and many other less notorious trials Joe built a reputation as one of the best lawyers in East or Southeast Texas. Goodwin had a thick head of long, white hair. He was more than six feet tall and about one big meal shy of 300 pounds but even larger than his physical traits; he had a legal reputation huge by even Texas standards.

When Linda was arrested she was not well known at the First Baptist Church of Nederland. Shortly after she was charged in the crime she became a regular there. Looking for heavenly answers to her earthly problems she talked to the pastor for his advice on legal matters. Her preacher recommended she fire Joe Goodwin and hire the good, Christian law team of Bill Howell and Helmut Erwing to defend her. Before the trial no one in Jefferson County other than Linda's pastor knew this legal team. Taking her preacher's advice, she fired Goodwin and hired Howell and Erwing. Among the reporters covering the trial the consensus was that if Howell and Erwing were a divine answer, apparently even God wanted to make sure Linda died by lethal injection.

Howell was the lead attorney. He had the physical stature of Goodwin, but not the legal stature. Like Goodwin, Howell was a huge man, also going well over six feet tall and most likely over 300 pounds as well. He had a world class beer gut. He is the only man I have ever seen with a tie more than a yard long. His ties needed to be extra long because they had to stretch more than a yard to cover the major girth between his neck and belt. With his physical makeup and outgoing personality he became a media favorite. He was jovial and always took time to answer all our questions. Whenever the questions got a little testy he kept his composure and gave some kind of answer, even if it was legalese that meant nothing.

Erwing was about six feet tall and very stocky. Both he and Howell looked like a decade earlier they could have played professional football. Like Howell, Erwing was always smiling and cooperative with the media. At first we found their amiability and accessibility quite helpful. As the trial proceeded we began to wonder if the smiles were a facade trying to cover up the fact that neither Howell nor Erwing had a clue as to what they should be doing to defend Linda.

On different occasions the legendary lawyer "Racehorse" Haynes tried cases in Jefferson County. I remember being almost as excited as the spectators in the court to see "Racehorse" in action. Big name lawyers with thousand dollar suits and flashy Rolex watches were nothing new to Beaumont. Howell and Erwing did not have big names, tailored clothes, fancy jewelry, or a legal reputation. And even in the legal backwaters of Jefferson County it soon became evident Linda was in trouble with this pair of "big city" lawyers representing her.

Early in the first hours of the trial I noticed that Erwing came in and out of the courtroom, handing papers to Howell and leaning over the railing to whisper things to him. For some reason it struck me as odd. The second day I had a "Eureka moment." Erwing never entered the lawyers' area of the courtroom. He always stayed in the public area of the courtroom, never as much as putting one foot inside the legal arena. Even during the breaks Howell would get up and walk over to Erwing so that Erwing never entered the area with the rest of the lawyers. I did not know much about law but I intuitively knew that something is wrong when the lawyer you have hired to represent you will not go beyond the railing that divides the public and the lawyers.

A courtroom is like any other arena. There are specific lines drawn delineating where the jury sits, where the judge sits, where the witnesses sit, and where the lawyers and the defendant sit. Outside those areas is where the public is allowed. Although at first glance a courtroom just looks like a large room with chairs, there are specified boundaries. If anyone violates those boundaries, they are escorted out by the bailiff. Do it again and you will find yourself in contempt of court and getting a few days lodging in the county jail.

After my "Eureka moment" I took advantage of the first break to go back in the judge's chambers, and out of earshot of any other reporter, talk with Judge Gist.

"What's with Erwing?"

"What do you mean?"

"He won't go inside the lawyers' area. He's in and out of the courtroom all day but he never sits down at the defense table with Howell and Burnett," I said. "Why won't he go into the lawyers' area?"

"Oh, I don't know," the judge answered. "But maybe if you called the state bar association in Austin they could give you a better idea about what's going on with him."

Suspecting Judge Gist was not-so-subtly trying to point me to something, I took his understated suggestion and at the lunch break went to the newsroom and called the Texas State Bar Association.

"He's what?!" I almost shrieked to the lady assisting me at the TSBA.

"He's disbarred," she repeated.

"Disbarred?" I asked in disbelief. "Then what's he doing in the courtroom?"

"Oh he can go in and out of the courtroom just like anyone else," she answered in her bureaucratic monotone. "He just can't represent anyone in court."

"So all he can do is be an errand boy relaying papers back and forth?"

"Sure. He just can't practice law for the next forty five days."

Of course when I put a microphone in front of Erwing and asked him about his legal status it all became a very trivial matter. Nothing serious. Just a question of legal interpretation, that is all. As if being represented in a mass murder trial by a disbarred attorney is no problem.

"It's just a technicality. In about a month it will all be over," Erwing assured me. And smiling like it was just a silly little trifle, "It's not permanent disbarment or anything like that. It's just a misunderstanding that will be over shortly."

It was "just a technicality" only in the sharp legal mind of Erwing. But after we made it our lead story that night the trial was interrupted and a hearing held to determine if Linda was represented by a legally licensed attorney. It could have been one of those "legal technicalities" that gets cases thrown out of court.

According to Erwing he had not completely lost his license. The state of Texas was just holding it for him for a while. You know, like a teenager is grounded for a while but will be back hanging out with the old gang in no time. As soon as he got the matter straightened out it would all be okay, according to Erwing.

Linda was on trial for her life and had an attorney on 45 days of suspension, plus 45 days of probation.

Linda was off to a flying start. She was accused of mass murder and her pastor hooked her up with an attorney fighting legal problems himself and without the right to practice law. When I questioned the lady at the bar association she said he was suspended because of inappropriate behavior in other legal proceedings and questions about money he owed some people. Neither she nor Erwing gave the specifics of what he did to get himself into legal limbo. According to Erwing; it was just legal technicalities that would be moot questions in 3 months. So other than him being a lawyer without a license, it was no problem. It may have been no problem for him but it compounded problems for Linda and potentially for the entire trial.

The strange events did not end with Erwing being on a legal leave of absence. Problems persistently dogged Linda and her legal eagles throughout the trial and every day along with the other reporters I wondered, "*What's next?*" The trial became a reporter's delight and nightmare. With Howell and Erwing you never knew what would happen next to stop the trial and take the entire story out of the courtroom and into the drama constantly surrounding them.

After the delay for the hearing on Erwing's qualifications, the trial barely resumed when another one of Howell and Erwing's misguided missiles came flying in from out of nowhere. One weekend shortly after the hearing on Erwing's legal status, someone stole his car. There were quite a few rumors and speculation circulating about the circumstances surrounding the car's disappearance, none of which were neatly put to rest by clear and concise explanations from either Howell or Erwing. And only with the legal team of Howell and Erwing could a totally separate incident such as a car theft once again threaten to get the case thrown out of court.

Erwing had his briefcase and all his legal papers about the

case in his car at the time it was stolen. The car disappeared in the early morning hours of a long Saturday night. Why his briefcase was in the car at the time was mystery. What happened to it after that is an even bigger mystery.

A few days later Erwing's briefcase and papers were mysteriously, or magically, found by a cross country traveler in central Texas. The person reportedly had gone to dump some trash in a roadside park trash can and saw the briefcase. The trash can was near a small town about 300 miles east of Houston. This Good Samaritan had retrieved the briefcase and contacted McGrath in the DA's office because McGrath and Jefferson County was written on almost every page. Erwing missed Monday's part of the trial as he drove almost 600 miles retrieving his stolen briefcase.

With all the side show circus shenanigans going on with her lawyers judge Gist decided to shore the team up a little bit to try to keep the case from ending up in a train wreck. Charles Carver, a Jefferson County attorney, was added to Linda's defense team. Unfortunately for Linda, Carver's arrival on the scene was after Howell and Erwing decided on one of the most curious defense maneuvers in legal history. Instead of questioning Linda, building their defense, discussing legal options, and preparing her for trial, they took her to a hypnotist. As odd a defense tactic as that was, even more puzzling, they took her back to people who would later be witnesses in the trial and asked them if they remembered her coming in and buying specific items that were used in the commission of the crime.

There were gasps of disbelief that turned to snickers from the reporters when these bits of information came to light during the trial. And during the breaks there were gut level laughs among us as we talked about the defense team sent from God. And when the questioning continued, it was sometimes difficult for me to keep from laughing out loud in court. I was not the only one shaking from stifled laughter while furiously scribbling in my reporter's notebook.

"Please state your name for the record," Flatten asked the witness.

"Fred Guzzardo," the man replied.

"Mr. Guzzardo, do you reside and do business in Jefferson County?"

"Yes I do,"

"What kind of business is that?"

"I own and operate Guzzardo's Feed Store in mid-county."

"Mr. Guzzardo have you ever seen the defendant in this case, Linda May Burnett in your store?" Flatten asked.

"Yes," he replied.

"When was that?"

"About a month ago."

"Was anyone with her?"

"Yes, a man."

"Do you know who that man was?"

"Well I do now. It was one of her attorneys, Mr. Erwing."

"Did they tell you why they had come to the store?"

"Yes."

"And could you please tell the court why they were there?"

"They were asking me questions about some rope. They wanted to know if I remembered Mrs. Burnett coming into my store and buying some rope."

What began as the perfect crime was now going wrong at every turn. Guzzardo did not remember Linda coming in the first time. But with her name in the papers in connection with the trial, her picture in every issue of the paper, and video of her on every channel on every newscast, he definitely remembered her coming in the second time. As you can imagine, seeing the most photographed and talked about woman in the history of Southeast Texas walk into your store was a bigger shock to Guzzardo than looking up and seeing the Governor of Texas walking through the door. There is no way Guzzardo could have forgotten her coming in the second time with her attorney. It was another subtle detail that somehow managed to slip by Howell and Erwing. I loved it. Howell and Erwing were good for a headline and lead story every day. For reporters, Howell and Erwing were the legal team from God.

Another strange twist that defied the law of probabilities was that Guzzardo's daughter, Karen, worked in the courthouse as a secretary for Judge Gist, about ten yards away from the judge, and also a short distance from the District Attorney's office. Every direction Howell and Erwing turned they made mistakes that cost them dearly during the trial. It seemed as if the State did not have the incriminating evidence, Howell and Erwing lead them to it -- an amazing theme that kept running through the trial. But even without what Howell and Erwing were uncovering, the State had an impressive array of circumstantial evidence already compiled.

The State continued building their case with Captain Hal Shaw. He was Captain of the Criminal Investigation Division with the Jefferson County Sheriff's Department and the first law officer to talk to Dugas the night of his arrest.

"Captain Shaw," Flatten began his line of questioning in the next phase of the trial. "When you went to the home of Joe Dugas in Port Neches the night of July seventh, did you have with you at that time a search warrant as well as a warrant for the arrest of Joe Dugas?"

"No, at that point we were just there to arrest him for kidnapping," he replied.

"Did you later get a search warrant?"

"Yes, the following day. The judge issued a search warrant and we went back to the house."

"Had you mentioned to Joe that you had a search warrant and would be going back to his house to take a look around for evidence?"

"Yes I did."

"And what did Joe tell you?"

"He said to go ahead and look around," Shaw answered in his nasal monotone. "He said he didn't have anything to hide."

"Did you in the course of the investigation perform a search of Joe's house Saturday, July eighth?"

"Yes, we did."

"I have here what is marked as State's exhibit "A". Have you ever seen these items before?"

"Yes, I have. We found them in a closet inside the house of Joe Dugas."

"Could you please describe to the court what these items are?"

"It's two pair of camouflage fatigues, the kind the military wears in combat."

There was a pause as Flatten submitted the fatigues as evidence. The pause was for the court reporter to mark them as a State's exhibit and enter them into evidence. With that done, Flatten continued, "Can you describe them?"

"Well one pair is a large pair. They're the size to fit a large man, at least six feet tall."

"What about the other pair?"

"They're much smaller."

"Would you say they would not fit the same person as the first pair?"

"No. They're for a much smaller person."

"The waist of the second pair of fatigues, it's about twenty five inches isn't it?"

"Yes."

Flatten held up the military gear to emphatically impress on the jury the petite size of the smaller set and that these were not just fatigues, but camouflage fatigues.

"Too small for Joe, but maybe small enough to fit someone about five feet tall and less than a hundred pounds? Someone much smaller than Joe Dugas?"

"Yes, definitely. There's no way Joe could have gotten into the second pair of fatigues."

"Do you think they would fit someone about the size of the

defendant, Linda Burnett?"

"Yes, I'd say they are for someone of a similar body type."

"Were there other items you found that evening at Joe's house?"

"Yes. We found a pair of black combat boots, a knife, two pair of handcuffs, tear gas, gun loading equipment, and a black leather slapper like police officers carry."

"Fatigues, combat boots, a slapper like police officers are authorized. Were you surprised to find these things at Joe's house?"

"No, not really."

"Why was that?"

"We were told the items were there and where he was keeping them."

"How did you know to expect these things at the house?"

"His brothers Richard and Roy told us. From the first few days after the murders Joe was telling them all kinds of details."

"Thank you. The State has no further questions. We pass the witness."

The DA's office at that point ratcheted up the drama by bringing Joe Dugas to the witness stand. I could feel the atmosphere of the courtroom dramatically shift when Joe began to testify. Before he took the stand I had heard from several law officers that Joe's bravado had quickly gotten the best of him. He had to tell someone even if it got him in trouble. Everyone had to know Joe Dugas really was as bad as Joe boasted. More than that, the perfection with which the crime was pulled off proved he was not only a bad ass, but a lot smarter than anyone had ever given him credit for. He was just a bar room brawler before. Now he was somebody.

One of the first persons Joe talked to after the trip to the grave was Calise Blanchard, an investigator for the Jefferson County District Attorney's office. Both Blanchard and Joe agreed that he confessed but after that their testimony was 180 degrees different. Blanchard said Joe initiated the talks by telling the jailers,

"I have something I want to talk about. It's about the Phillips family."

When Joe had his turn on the witness stand the story became one of confession forced by verbal and physical abuse from Jefferson County Investigator Russell Landry, Chambers County Deputy Robert Ogden, and Blanchard. Dugas testified that jailers and investigators beat him, drugged him, and forced him to go to the grave site. Dugas contended that he was threatened not only by Blanchard, but by Linda.

After spending hundreds and hundreds of hours in court covering all kinds of trials, this was the best. It was fun to be in the courtroom and exciting to go on the air. As I did my live shots from the courthouse I knew that all over Southeast Texas jaws were dropping and people were letting out audible gasps as I outlined the details of the testimony. Every day the trial became more and more incredible. For complete coverage the newspaper reporters had the edge because they could go on and on about the intricate details of each day's revelations. For TV and radio reporters our challenge was to get the story under two minutes of air time while stuffing in as many of the mind-boggling details as possible.

According to Joe he was a victim of forces greater than himself, a massive police conspiracy. First he said deputies took his hand and forced him to sign a confession. In his confession he said he and Linda dug the grave and she sent him back after the baby. He said he heard shots. When he got back with the baby the four adults were dead. He said Linda then put the rifle in his hands, pointed it at the baby and forced his hand to pull the trigger.

Joe confessed that: "I closed my eyes and I don't remember where the baby was shot. I don't remember much after I put the baby down."

There was some testimony to support Joe's claim coercion was used to get his confession. Jailers and law officers who had access to Dugas testified they saw bruises and scrapes on him. The sheriff's office had pictures of Joe looking battered. Joe said his battering came from Blanchard.

At the first recess after the testimony I cornered McGrath. I had interviewed Blanchard several times and found him to always be a totally dedicated and honest lawman, which I said to McGrath. "I don't understand it. I don't believe Blanchard beat a confession out of him, but why was he roughed up?"

"He did that himself," McGrath said, a most serious look on his face.

Not knowing much about what goes on inside a jail, I said, "Huh? Run that by me again. He beat himself up? How can you beat yourself up?"

"It's nothing new," McGrath answered as if he was letting me in on some confidential inside information. "Prisoners do it all the time. It gives them a way out from their confession and it maintains their macho mindset that they did not just spill their guts without a fight. Joe was beating his head against the bars. That's how he got all black and blue. Nine o'clock Saturday night we had to have a doctor go in and give him a sedative. He was really banging himself up and we had to calm him down."

McGrath switched gears to how important the confession was, coerced or given freely. "If he hadn't talked we'd have never made a case against him. We had nothing. Without the bodies, anything he'd told his brothers was just hearsay. He knew that."

After the break Calise Blanchard took the stand. He said Joe started talking and cooperated every step of the way. Blanchard testified that on Sunday evening July 9th Joe took Sheriff Pounds, Jefferson County Investigator Russell Landry and other investigators out to Gilbert Woods on Highway 365, about a half mile west of Interstate 10. It was 7 o'clock, but in July that still gave them more than an hour of daylight to start scouring the area around the graves for clues and recovering the bodies. Joe showed them where to find the bodies. Once certain the bodies were where Joe showed them they quickly took him back to the Chambers County jail and arraigned him on murder charges.

As Blanchard went into his testimony of what happened I had my pen in hand waiting for details I knew would be part of my story. Blanchard delivered with stunning details that brought gasps from the audience and even made the reporters squirm in our seats.

"At first he took us to a spot where he thought they were buried," Blanchard testified. "Then he said, 'this isn't right,' and we searched a little longer. Finally he led us to a spot and said, 'this looks right.'"

"Did it look like a grave?"

"No. Not at all. It was perfectly hidden. We never would have found it if he hadn't pointed it out to us."

"What did you do next?"

"Rather than just start digging, Russell Landry, one of the investigators at the scene, stuck a rod into the ground where Joe said they were buried. When he pulled it up, we could smell the bodies. We knew we had found them."

That little bit of forensic insight drew looks of disgust from all over the courtroom, including some from the jury box.

"Was there any other physical evidence recovered from the scene?"

"We found seven twenty-two caliber long-rifle shells within ten feet of the grave."

"Did you find any personal belongings, any identification on the bodies?"

"None. There was some rope around their wrists, and some tape, but no identification."

"And other than the rope around their wrists, were there any other signs they were taken there against their will?"

"There was tape on the mouths and around the heads of Ester, the grandmother, and Martha, and some tape on Elmer's head."

I barely had time to make notes and try to wipe the disgusting images out of my head when the State called its next expert witness. From past trials I knew that the drama is often sucked out of the courtroom when the State's expert witnesses go over the details of a crime scene. Just establishing a chain of possession on the evidence can run for 15 minutes or more and be as boring as watching mold grow. Expert witnesses are usually mechanical in their description and in their delivery of details. They are pros and know that their "Just the facts. Nothing but the facts," approach will leave very little room for cross-examination and get them off the witness stand as quickly as possible. Meanwhile there are few objections the defense can raise because the description of the physical evidence of the crime scene leaves little room for debate. The defense can only object to something of a procedural nature, such as the State asking a question that would require conjecture about events, or when the State is leading the witness rather than asking questions. Silent for most of the testimony, Linda and her attorneys listened as Dr. LeBurr followed Blanchard's testimony with his description of the crime scene. Dr. LeBurr was the medical doctor and forensic pathologist for the State who was also at the grave for the exhumation of the bodies.

Flatten began the questioning. "Dr. LeBurr, could you tell the court how; in your opinion the victims were murdered?"

"Jason, the three year old, was the second victim taken out of the grave," the doctor began slowly as though it were just another trial and another testimony. "He was shot once through the right eye, and once on the top, rear part of his skull."

"What did you rule as cause of death?"

"Two gunshot wounds to the head."

"And what about the other victims?"

"The two grandparents, Ester and Bishop, were also killed by two gunshot wounds to the head, once in the eye and once from the top of the head in the rear. Elmer, their son, was shot once in the head. His wife Martha was shot once in the right eye and once in the temple."

"Using your knowledge and the location of the entrance wounds, how would you describe the position of the victims and the murderer?"

"By the angle of trajectory, they were apparently in the grave and the person doing the shooting standing above them firing at a downward angle. At the angle of their wounds, Bishop and Ester were probably shot in the grave in a standing position."

"How far away from the victims would you say the person doing the shooting stood?"

"I would say the muzzle of the gun was about ten inches away from the heads of the victims."

"Were you able to determine what type of weapon was used?"

"It was a small caliber, high velocity weapon."

"Could a twenty-two caliber high velocity bullet cause such an injury?"

"Yes, that would be what you would expect from a twenty-two."

"Doctor LeBurr, if you could for the court, describe the condition of the bodies when they were recovered?"

"The bodies were in an advanced state of decomposition."

"You testified they were all killed by gunshot wounds to the head. Was there any other evidence of physical harm to the victims?"

"All of them were clothed, except for the grandfather. He was wearing only his shirt. For some reason one of the old man's testicles had been distorted. The body was too badly decomposed for an analysis to determine how or why that happened."

The courtroom was packed to the max. After the revelation about the old man's testicles I quickly looked to the jury box and then audience to get everyone's reaction. The jury remained pretty stoic but there were looks of horror in the audience, except from Linda's husband Leo, who was in court every day and never revealed any emotion. It was obvious everyone in the audience was nauseated and did not try to hide it from registering on their faces. In this trial rather than saying "the spectators made gasps when it was revealed that..." I kept a daily tally of how many times it happened and often used the count for filler and drama in my 6 o'clock news reports.

Flatten did not flinch with the revelation. Instead he paused for dramatic effect, and to let the words sink deeply into the minds of the jurors to paint a permanent picture of Linda as a heinous and inhumane person. When he was satisfied the picture was there, and that the gasps from the audience had fully registered with the jury, he continued. "Dr. LeBurr, could you describe for the court how the bodies were positioned in the grave?"

"The old man was towards the rear and the bottom of the grave. The grandmother was next to and partially on top of him. Next to her was the daughter-in-law. Then in the front of the grave were the son, Elmer, and the 3-year-old on him."

"And, in what position was the child found?"

"On top. With his right arm locked around his father's neck."

There were again gasps from the audience and some tears as spectators tried to muffle the sound of their crying with tissues over their mouths. My gut reaction matched the crowd but my mind was also on my story and my watch. There was no doubt. I knew I had my lead sentence for the six o'clock news.

And at six, live from the courthouse, I began, "With his right arm locked around his father's neck..."

CHAPTER NINE

The Plan

"What was going on with them? Was this their idea of a good time?" I asked McGrath. "We still don't know why they wanted to kill them. Were they doing it for pure meanness or was there some other ulterior motive?"

"Yes, they're that mean," McGrath answered. "But they didn't do it just for kicks. Joe had it in his mind that he was settling a score. And there was more to it. They had it all planned out."

"So what was their big plan?" I asked, unsatisfied with the tidbits he was offering.

"You're going to be covering the trial aren't you?" he asked without any change of facial expression, or answering my question.

"Sure," I answered.

"Then just show up everyday and we'll tell you the whole story," he assured me with a sly grin.

"Yeah, the whole story according to the DA's office?" I replied with a look of skepticism.

"Nope," he said. "You'll be surprised who will be telling the story, and it won't be coming from my office."

"Okay. Cute. But could you be a little more definitive than that?" I asked.

"Nope. Just be there," McGrath answered. He walked off signaling that was all the information I would get out of him. He did not want to make headlines that day but he had the appearance of being very certain about himself.

As a reporter I loved this trial. All the characters were better than anything I could make up or embellish. McGrath was always the cocky Bantam rooster strutting about. Flatten was stoic with his face giving an image of all the details of the prosecution being played out behind his eyes. The defense was smiling, with an air of confidence that the case would break down, the judge would declare a mistrial, and it would all be over. I had covered many trials but this was at the top of the list for drama being played out with a cast of characters better than a Hollywood casting director could have assembled. And what a script. It had it all. Cheatin', sex, sadism, murder, double-cross, confessions, and choreographed by bumbling attorneys, with Cajun music from the Rodair Club playing in the background.

The trial was more intriguing every day and with every bit of new information added to the record. Between the arraignments, grand jury indictments, and preliminary motions I watched as a parade of witnesses took turns on the stand painting a very ugly and convincing picture about the brutality of Joe. Joe was still the central character in the case even though we were learning more and more about Linda. Joe was coming off so bad that he would give anyone around him the stench of evil. I had the feeling that was exactly the message the DA's office was trying to subliminally send to the jury.

It was a great trial to cover. Just calling back to the newsroom during the courtroom breaks was a treat because they knew every day brought new surprises. Every time I went on the air I knew people stopped whatever they were doing to make sure they did not miss any detail. It was that compelling. Stories like this do not come along very often for reporters, and I savored every syllable I spoke. The trial kept getting more compelling and more steeped into the area's roots every day, especially when the trial took another turn, into the night life of Joe, Linda, and the Rodair club. The club had already been mentioned several times during the trial but the next turn of testimony took us through the doors and into the middle of the dance floor.

Joe Thibedeaux was the club's manager. The Rodair Club is the best known club among Cajuns in Southeast Texas for hearing the purest, best, and nothing but, Cajun music. Thibedeaux was unadulterated Cajun and caretaker to the French flavored music the Acadians brought with them when they settled in Southeast Texas. You hear them referred to as Acadians but more commonly, Cajun. Among friends they will even answer to the term used most frequently to describe them, 'coonass.' No one is sure exactly where the moniker came from, but it is the one you hear most often to describe those of Acadian descent.

I grew up in South Texas, 7 miles north of Mexico. Southeast Texas was like another country to me. The flavor of South Texas is salsa, in Southeast Texas it is crawfish etouffee. South Texas has its famous and infamous whereas the Beaumont and Port Arthur areas are known for football players and the different ethnic groups that settled the area. The Dutch established the city of Nederland when they settled between Beaumont and Port Arthur. There is even a large windmill downtown commemorating the area's roots. Besides the windmill Nederland is known as the home of the Ritters. At the time of the trial, one owned a lumber store in Nederland next to the Twin City Highway. Another Ritter left to go into business in Beaumont and later become the city's mayor. But the most famous Ritter, Tex, went to Hollywood and made cowboy movies, became "America's Most Beloved Cowboy," and father to John Ritter of "Three's Company" fame. Tex Ritter is once again a permanent resident of Nederland; his grave is in the

Oak Bluff Memorial Park cemetery overlooking the Neches River.

There are not any famous Cajuns that come to mind, maybe A.J. Judice, aka, the Crazy Cajun, but when you look in the phone book, the main ethnic imprint in the area will be found under various spellings of names like Beaudreau, Theriot, Martineau, LeBlanc, Judice, Guidry, Thibedeaux, or Richard, pronounced Ree-shard when used as a last name.

If there is any particular ethnic group that typifies Southeast Texas and gives the area a uniqueness all its own, it is the Cajuns. They were run out of France and settled in Canada, where they got the name Acadians. They did not find Canada all that hospitable either and migrated south. When they reached the Gulf coast along both sides of the Texas-Louisiana border they finally found the climate and surroundings that suited them. Cajuns as a general rule are very good natured and take a lot of ribbing about their heritage. They are a fun group of people. For many years they have been an important part in operating the huge oil refineries in Port Arthur. When they are not working they are most likely to be found fishing on the bayou, crabbing at Sabine Pass, or dancing at the Rodair Club. They are as much a part of Southeast Texas as the crawfish, alligators, and mosquitoes.

The Rodair Club was the adopted home of Joe Dugas and for about 3 months before the Phillips family disappeared, Linda's as well. It was a good place to hear music heavy with accordion and zydeco sounds laced with French lyrics. It was a great place to get as good a bowl of file' gumbo or a plate of crawfish etouffee as you can get between Houston and New Orleans. The French flavor along with plenty of honky-tonk atmosphere made it a natural hangout for Joe.

All of the flavor and atmosphere of the Cajun contribution to Southeast Texas was on the witness stand when the State called its next witness, Joe Thibedeaux. A grin broke out on my face with his first few syllables. He was as Cajun as they come. You could almost hear the zydeco accordion playing in the background as he spoke.

Flatten began the questioning for the State. "Mr. Thibedeaux have you ever heard of the codefendant in this case, a Mr. Joe Dugas?"

"For sure," Thibedeaux answered back with his thick French inflection. All the reporters were smiling at his heavy accent even though all of us had heard it many times around the mid-county and Port Arthur area. Although we were smiling we were all wondering how to convey the earnestness of his testimony without speaking in dialect ourselves, and on occasion wondering how we were going to translate some of the testimony when his brogue got really Cajun.

"For a long time he used to hang out around da club," Thibedeaux began his testimony.

"Did he ever work for you as an employee of the Rodair Club?"

"Oh yeah, for sure."

"How did he come to be employed? Did you ask him to work there?"

"He asked me if he can help out, help keep da things in order. He was always dere and he's a big burly guy who has a 'don't mess wid me,' look about him, so I think, okay, and I hire him to be da bouncer."

"Did you ever have occasion to fire Joe from that job?"

"Yeah, just a few months after I put him on da payroll."

"Could you tell the court why you fired him?"

"I was afraid I gonna get sued."

"Why? What would make you be afraid of a lawsuit?"

"Joe was trouble," Thibedeaux tilted his head to the right, raised his left eyebrow, and launched into a story. "One night we had a customer who was causing some problems. Joe decide it was time for da guy to leave. But he didn't just ask da guy to leave. Oh no, not Joe. Joe, he start a fight with da guy. Da guy just a kid, name Guidry."

Flatten and McGrath sat there letting Thibedeaux ramble on.

The defense sat across the aisle waiting for some point to interrupt with an objection but in his slow, methodical pace Thibedeaux told about Joe's last night on the payroll.

"Joe pick da kid up and lift da kid over his head and throw him to da floor. Joe alot bigger and stronger dan da guy and Joe pin him on da floor. Joe had him down on da floor and was hitting him something hard. Dere was not one thing between Joe's big fists and da floor except dis guy's head. I tell you for sure, Joe hit Guidry so hard he break his right hand. We had to pull Joe from da guy. I tell you, Joe would have killed da guy for sure if we hadn't stopped him."

"Was that the only incident of that nature while Joe was employed by you?" Flatten asked with his chin down and eyebrows raised to Thibedeaux on the stand.

"Nooo," Thibedeaux drawled out his reply steeped in a Cajun flavor as thick as a crawfish pie. "One other time he got cross wid a customer, just a kid. Nothing happen at da club but dat don't mean nothin to Joe, Joe go follow him home. He go and he get in a fight with da kid in da kid's own front yard. Da kid's old man come out da house and Joe go to fightin him too. I knew dat was too much. Joe just wanna fight. He always gotta do things his way. He don't need no ex-cuse."

"So these incidents prompted you to get rid of Joe?"

"For sure. Joe a time bomb. You never know when he gonna explode. All you know was dat trouble was certain as long as Joe round da place."

"After you terminated Joe as an employee, was that the last you saw of Joe."

"No. Joe would always be round. I couldn't tell him he couldn't come in da place. I could just tell him if he wants to fight he got to fight on his own. He can fight if he wants but not if he gonna work for me, for sure. No, nothin change. Joe still there at da club just as much. Only difference now I don't pay him to be dere."

"Did you ever see him at the club with the defendant, Linda

May Burnett?"

"For sure, two, three time a week. Every weekend."

"And how did Joe refer to Linda when she was with him at the Rodair Club?"

"Aw, Joe, he always talking about she his girlfriend."

"Did you ever see Joe with Linda May Burnett and Charlie Neal?"

"Oh yeah," Thibedeaux drawled out with emphasis. "Dey spend a lot of time at my club."

"Do you recall when was the last time you saw the three of them together at your club?"

"Joo-ly first. Da day dem people killed."

"Thank you Mr. Thibedeaux. We have no further questions your honor."

What great testimony. I could not have asked for better. There were at least a half dozen reporters in the court every day and I could feel the creative juices flowing through our section. Every reporter had a notebook in one hand and pen in the other, ready for the next startling revelation. Every witness painted a more vivid and damning image of Joe. The State was doing a great job of connecting the dots between Joe, Linda, and trouble.

One of the biggest dots to be connected was another headline maker. It was the confession Linda signed shortly after her arrest and before she had a lawyer and it was the State's next plank in the gallows they were constructing for her. Linda signed the confession which allowed the State to admit it into evidence. Later, when she was on the witness stand, and asked if it was her signature, she took the Fifth Amendment.

According to her testimony when she was called to testify and asked about the confession, she said she asked for a lawyer several times but was refused each time. She said the officers told her she would not need an attorney until after she gave them a statement. It was her testimony that they never read her the Miranda Rights or allowed her to use the telephone. She also testified she never voluntarily or freely gave the confession marked "State's exhibit #7." Exhibit #7 was a confession made to the sheriff's deputies signed after two a.m. July eighth, one week after the murders and the day before she was interrogated by the FBI and given a polygraph test. She gave them another confession signed July tenth.

It was her confession given to the state that McGrath wanted entered into the record. It began, *"I was crying as we reached the point of parking the cars on the night of the murders. It took several minutes for Joe to calm me down enough to continue."*

From there her statement went into the details about her and Joe changing clothes next to the car, taking off their civilian clothing, changing into military style fatigues, and putting black on their faces.

"We got out, got the rifle out of the back seat. We had everything in the back seat. Joe said we don't have any choice, let's go in and get it over with."

"I was very edgy going into the house. The old man was very mean. Joe grabbed up the baby and told them to be still, he just wanted to ask them some questions." She said that Joe using the baby was unexpected and upsetting to her. *"That made me so mad that I took the baby from Joe. When that happened the old man got angry and jumped up. Joe hit him in the head with his pistol. Joe had the old man on the floor and I held a gun on the other three."*

According to the statement they then handcuffed Martha, Bishop, and Elmer and tied Ester with rope. Bishop was bleeding bad so they looked around the house, found a pillow case and cleaned it up.

"The baby was crying and I was loving him. I got Joe to get something for the old man's head. It was inhuman. I didn't like what was happening. Then Joe tied up the girl and I put the gun to Elmer's head. I said talk fast or you'll look worse than the old man."

"It was hot but I was cold and sweating. I knew that Joe would kill them and maybe me too. The girl asked if they were going

to die and I told her they had some pictures they were going to blackmail them with. I told her she'd better pray. I got very nervous, I was afraid. I knew it was wrong."

After subduing the four adults, she said they forced them into their car, the four adults in one car with Joe driving, and Linda following in her car with the baby. From the Phillips' farmhouse they drove to the grave site, approximately ten miles away. At the grave her statement read, *"I opened the gate. It hurt my back. I had the check stubs and photographs. At the grave he taped their mouths."*

"I was mad at Joe. I didn't like the way Joe looked at me. Something was very wrong. It was very cruel. Joe looked strange. That's when I decided I was going to let Joe put them in the grave and then I'd shoot Joe."

"The old man tried to give Joe some trouble and Joe told him where to get off at. Joe told him he'd never given him anything but trouble and he was trying to blackmail Joe and that's what led to the trouble they were in."

"Joe took the needles and gave them shots of something that smelled like roach poison. He said it would put them to sleep and ease the pain. We took all the jewelry and identification off of them in case they were dug up.

"He made the old man and woman get in the grave and told me to shoot them."

"I wanted to kill Joe and myself. Joe pointed the gun at them and he told me to shoot and I shot them. I closed my eyes and shot them. I looked one time and I couldn't stand it. The gun was about 8-10 inches away from them. They were shot in the head. Then he took the gun and shot them again."

"He made the other two get in the grave and he shot them. I couldn't do it. Joe slapped me hard. I was quiet and cold. I couldn't think. Joe shot them a lot of times."

"He went after the baby to kill it. I was trying to pull the baby away from him. I said, 'Joe, please don't do this.' Joe threw

the baby in the grave and shot him. I couldn't stand it. I sat there while he covered up the grave. I couldn't help. He hit me and told me to come to my senses. I was afraid of him.'"

"I screamed. I could still see the baby in the grave. I felt sick leaving the grave."

At this point everyone in court room was sick. I had heard many hours of courtroom testimony, including murder cases but this was some of the most compelling and disgusting description I had ever heard. The reporters section was directly across the courtroom from the jury. Although the jury members rarely looked at us during testimony, I could feel every reporter trying to maintain a poker face to keep from influencing the jury. I hoped the other reporters were doing a better job than me. It was not easy with an image of that small child thrown on top of the adults and then shot through the head. Not only were the five killed, they were tortured with an injection of poison before killing them. What was really sick was that after injecting them with roach poison, shooting them through the head execution style was the most compassionate part of the crime.

My eyes scanned the jury. They were not as able to keep their emotions off their faces, especially some of the women jurors. The State had done an excellent job of getting into the record a very disturbing and heinous mental image of that night at the gravesite. And the rest of the confession painted a picture of a crime intricately planned out, down to the minutest of details. Minute, sickening details. In the audience there were sounds of sniffling noses and muffled crying.

"We put everything in the car and double checked to make sure there was nothing anywhere. We brushed our tracks down. I couldn't think. All I could think about was he killed that baby."

"We took their car to a bridge and checked to make sure no one was around. It was a white shell road. We took towels and wiped that car down real good. Then we pushed it in the ditch."

"We went back to the Phillips house. I wanted the cops to

catch us and shoot us right there. Joe looked in the ice box for something to eat. We cleaned up the house and cleaned off prints from everything we touched."

"After that we went back to the Rodair Club. Joe was still telling me to get hold of myself. We threw the watches and rings in Twin Lakes. Joe kept the money out of the billfolds. We took all their stuff and wiped it clean and threw it away."

"Joe threw a bag of their stuff in the water and it floated. He shot it several times with a shotgun and it sank. I burned the photos and checks and flushed them down the commode."

"I tried to blank it all out. I was afraid Joe wouldn't hold up. I was the stronger of the two of us."

"After I got out of jail I found a twenty-two cartridge in the car door. It scared the hell out of me. The cops had been all over that car. The bullet was wedged between the window and the door. We rolled down the window and got it out. Joe got paranoid about me and the cops. He called me and I told him not to worry."

"The Phillips were blackmailing him. He just wanted them to leave him alone."

To verify the validity of the confession, Jay White, a female deputy sheriff present for the questioning of Linda was called to the witness stand. She said Linda freely agreed to give the confession and to sign it. At this point Flatten sat as McGrath took over the questioning. "Officer White, why did she tell you she was making the statement?"

"She said that she hadn't committed any crime. She gave the statement without any of us in the interrogation area asking any questions. She said she hadn't done anything and wanted to tell her (Deputy White) about it."

Before talking with the sheriff's office FBI agents also interrogated Linda. When they asked her about the night of July first she said she and Joe went out to his house and "messed around" and then left to go to the beach. She told the FBI interrogators she and Joe came back from the beach and she left his house about two

Sunday morning.

Every day Linda appeared in court very well dressed in an outfit different from the day before. Although a middle class housewife, her wardrobe approved significantly after the trial began. Once again she was wearing a very nice dress that did not look like something bought off the rack. And around her neck was another new, brightly colored scarf to accessorize her outfit. Topping off her ensemble was a light-brown wig, one of several she wore during the trial.

Each outfit she wore had one central feature, an attractive scarf around the neck. The only variation to her appearance was the pair of dark horn rimmed glasses she would take out and put on to read when there was something entered in the record that included a transcript of testimony. Linda was small, frail, had almost no figure and was not physically attractive. Her face was very pitted from what appeared to be a severe case of teenage acne. But with the wardrobe and makeup advice from the attorneys, she put on her best face every day for court.

As her statement to officer White was read into the record Linda took that day's matching scarf from around her neck and used it to wipe away the tears as the words became an official part of the trial.

The confession was now a part of the record so the State's next move was to call Linda to the witness stand. She gave a much different account of her confession. By this point in the trial Charles Carver was clearly the lead defense attorney and doing all the questioning. And it was evident the defense had some major damage control problems. Carver immediately went to work trying to make the jury believe the confession was coerced, a difficult thing to do because Linda took the fifth when the State asked if it was her signature on the confession.

"Why did you sign this statement?" Carver began.

"They told me they wanted a statement right then," Linda testified. "They told me they wanted a statement or they would take me back to the grave and put me in it."

"Who made these statements to you?" Carver asked.

On the verge of tears, Linda replied, "Captain Hal Shaw. He asked me how I liked the odor of dead people."

"Were you ever made aware of your rights or allowed to have an attorney present during this interrogation?"

"No. Never. I wanted to call someone but I was told I was under arrest and had no rights."

Beginning to cry, Linda said, "Calise Blanchard said it was a matter of life or death."

"What did you think he meant by that?"

"I thought they'd kill me if I didn't sign something right then," Linda said sniffling and wiping her nose with an ever-present wadded up tissue.

"Did the officers there tell you what would happen if you signed the statement?"

"They said all I had to do was sign it and I could go home."

"And after you gave them the statement what did they tell you to do?"

"I was told to initial it, Officer White took the statement but never let me read it."

"Did you initial it?"

"Yes."

"Did you know what was in that statement?"

"No."

"Why not?"

"I never read it."

"If you never read it, why did you sign it?"

"I signed it because I thought it would save my life," she answered through tears streaming down her face. "The whole room was filled with the smell of death."

"Linda," Carver asked in a consoling voice, "Were you involved with the death of the Phillips family?"

"No," she responded crying and her voice breaking. "I have

never killed anyone, not even an animal."

"No further questions, your honor. We pass the witness."

McGrath was unfazed by everything that had just transpired and was anxiously ready for his turn to question Linda. He rose from the table and approached Linda with the confession in his hand. "Mrs. Burnett, if you'll look at the evidence marked State's exhibit number seven; do you see a signature on the bottom of it?"

"Yes," she curtly answered.

"Is that your signature?"

"On the advice of my attorney I plead the fifth amendment,"

"No further questions your honor," McGrath addressed the court with a very confident, almost cocky, inflection in his voice.

The bailiff stepped in and moved the microphone away from Linda. Without looking at the jury, she stepped down and walked back to her seat at the long, very dark oak, defense table. Like all the other furniture in the courtroom the defense table was massive and looked like it would take four men and at least two dollies to move it. And at more than 3 feet wide, it also served as a formidable and psychological barrier to discourage an angry witness from jumping off the stand to attack the defendant.

With Linda back at the table Carver rose to speak to the court. At this point Carver was doing all the talking for the defense and rarely leaning over to Howell to ask questions or seek advice. Once to his feet Carver objected to the statements and her confession being admitted into evidence. When Judge Gist asked for Carver's legal reason he said that at the time only Dugas had been arrested and yet they were focusing on Linda as a participant. He insisted she was denied her rights because they were questioning her as a witness and that it is not normal procedure to ask a witness to take a polygraph test. According to Carver's line of legal reasoning a polygraph test is normally used for suspects, not witnesses.

Judge Gist listened to his appeal and quickly denied his motion to suppress admission of the confession. Carver slowly sat back down, literally and figuratively like a balloon slowly deflating.

From Linda's testimony the trial shifted to Charles Neal. Neal was married to Joe's cousin and was also one of his honky-tonk buddies. Neal was used as a prop to support both the State and defense cases. The defense wanted to instill doubt in the jurors' minds about Linda's participation. They wanted the jury to focus on Neal as a cohort of Joe's and the person who was with him that night helping him kill the five. The defense was trying to get the jury to think of killing five people something only men do. They wanted the jury to think of mass murder as a job for two strong men, not a man and a five foot, ninety eight pound woman.

On the other side the State used Neal to bolster their case as well. They wanted Neal's testimony to prove that it was Linda and Joe responsible for the entire plot and that the two of them had been thinking about murdering the Phillips and planning how to do it for a long time. Neal looked to be forty-something, with a lean, muscular build, the age and body type of a person you would want to have along with you if you needed to subdue five people and then dispose of five bodies.

When the State called Neal to the witness stand he came into the court wearing a plaid shirt with a sports coat, but no tie. He looked as out of place in the sports coat as he did in court. You could see he was very uncomfortable with both. I could not help but feel a little bit sorry for him. I knew how uncomfortable I felt just testifying about the news coverage our station gave the trial.

Flatten began the questioning for the State and started in a soft, reassuring voice to try to calm Neal. He began with some easy, non-threatening questions to help him settle down. "Mr. Neal, how long have you known Joe Dugas?"

"Oh, I'd say about five to six years," Neal nervously began.

"Mr. Neal, did you ever have an occasion to talk with Joe about killing his ex-in-laws?"

"Yeah, he talked to me about it."

"What did he say?"

"He said he wanted me to help him kill his ex-in-laws. He said they were a thorn in his side and he wanted to get rid of them."

"That's it? Because they were a thorn in his side?"

"Well, he also said they were hiding Mary, his wife,"

"Was this the only occasion Joe mentioned killing his former in-laws?"

"No, there was another time."

"When was that?"

"It was on May twenty ninth, Memorial Day. I remember it because it was just before Joe and I went to summer camp for the reserves," Neal elaborated.

"Could you please tell the court where that conversation took place, Mr. Neal?" Flatten asked with a piercing tone in his voice.

"At the Rodair Club."

"Was there anybody else with him at that time?"

"Yeah, it was Linda."

"For the record Mr. Neal, Linda May Burnett who was with Joe that day at the Rodair Club, is she in the courtroom today?"

"Yes, she's here," Neal said, although not looking at her or acknowledging her presence.

"And for the record Mr. Neal," Flatten continued as he maneuvered to get Linda positively identified and placed at the Rodair Club with Joe, "could you point out the person in the courtroom who was with Joe and introduced to you as Linda May Burnett."

As every witness before him Neal raised his hand and pointed at Linda. The State was doing a good job of getting every person on the witness stand to start with "Yup, that's her," and I could sense the repetition of this gesture was registering with the jury. Another person on the stand, another, "Yup, that's her."

"She's right there at the defense table," Neal said with his right hand extended and index finger pointing to Linda. His eyes quickly shifted away from her back to Flatten. "She's the woman sitting next to her attorney, Mr. Carver. She's at his left hand side."

"That was the last time you saw Joe Dugas along with the defendant, Linda May Burnett together at the Rodair Club?"

"That's right," Neal answered.

I could hear the relief in his voice as he realized at this point the State was directing its focus away from him and towards Linda. By this time the Rodair club had become such a central part of the trial I just used the letter "R" as my shorthand way of mentioning it in my notes.

"When you met the defendant, how did Joe introduce her to you?"

"Joe said, "this is the lady that's going to help me kill my in-laws in Winnie.""

Flatten paused a moment to let the last sentence sink in with the jury. He knew he was getting to the most incriminating part of Neal's testimony, so he looked at Neal with a puzzled look on his face to set up the next question. "And did Mrs. Burnett have any response to the statement that she was going to help him commit murder?"

"She said, 'and he's going to help me kill my ex-old man.'"

"Do you have any idea why Joe would bring up such a strange topic to introduce you to her?" Flatten said, tilting his head to the left and rolling his eyes up and to the right as if he were searching his mind for some kind of rationale for this peculiar introduction of Linda.

"He had talked with me several times about killing his in-laws,"

I could hear the discomfort in Neal's voice and could feel his uneasiness as he felt himself being drawn back into the details of the crime and giving up testimony he knew could mean the execution of both Joe and Linda.

"Did you ever have occasion to go with him out to their house?"

"Yeah, once he took me out to their house and we drove by

it. He drove on a little bit and parked the car on the road. Then he got out of the car and he walked back to the house and up to a window."

"What did he say about the incident when he got back to the car?"

"He said, '"if I'd of had a gun I could have killed them all.'"

Dropping that line of questioning, Flatten went another direction. "When you were there at the Rodair with Joe and Linda did she go into details about why she was going to help him kill his former in-laws?"

"Yeah, she said after she helped him kill his in-laws he was going to help her kill her ex-old man."

"Did she tell you the name of former husband?"

"Yeah, Hubert Miller."

Flatten tilted his head to the right and eyes to the left towards Neal and asked, "Did she give any specifics as to why she would want to kill him?"

"Linda said she wanted him dead because he wasn't paying child support. There was apparently bad blood between them. She said she had shot at him before and he had taken some shots at her."

"She said she wanted him dead just because he wasn't paying any child support?"

"No, she said she wanted his social security benefits for her kids."

"Did she offer any incentive to anyone who'd get rid of Hubert?"

"She said she'd pay his fifty thousand dollars worth of insurance money to anyone who'd kill him."

"The State has no further questions your honor. Your honor, the State calls Gloria Blanchard to the stand."

Among Joe's more civilized pastimes was playing in a band. Gloria Blanchard's husband played in the same band. Shortly after the Phillips family disappeared she had a conversation with Joe about Linda. Joe and Gloria's husband were playing for a dance at the Senior Citizens' Center in Port Arthur. She testified she had seen Linda there at the same time and Joe talked about Linda and his in-laws. This was getting more and more stupefying to me. Yes, they committed the perfect crime. The plan was intricately conceived and perfectly carried out. But the only way Joe could have been less subtle about it would have been to put an ad in the paper saying he did it and where they were buried.

Gloria took the stand and immediately began telling a revealing conversation she had with Joe.

"He said his in-laws were missing."

"Did he say anything else about them at that time?"

"Yes, I knew they used to be his in-laws and everybody was speculating about whether they would find them alive or not. I asked him and he said, 'no they're not alive.'"

"And this would have been before their bodies had been discovered?"

"Yes. It was almost a week before they found them."

"Did he say anything that would indicate him being implicated in their deaths?" Flatten asked with his head tilted slightly to the right and his left eyebrow arched.

"He said he had an alibi. He said, "I was with a woman at the beach."

"Did you ask who that woman was?"

"I asked if it was Linda and he said, 'how'd you know,' and I told him I just figured it was her since she was there with him."

"And did he say anything more that day about Linda?"

"He said she'd testify for him in court. He said she'd testify they went to the beach. He said Leo (Linda's husband) knew where they were at and he even helped them clean sand out of the car after they got back."

Pens were flying all down the row of reporters. The State was into the heart of the evidence and very carefully constructing a very damning case against Linda, using an impressive array of building materials supplied by Joe's gift of gab. From Gloria's testimony the State moved the focus of the investigation to Linda and Leo's house. At Joe's house the State built its case on the things they found. At Linda's house the State focused on what they did not find. Investigators found a car and shovels but not as much as a hair or speck of dirt to link her to the crime. The State took the offense on that lack of evidence and worked to turn it from a negative into a positive. It began with Captain Hal Shaw on the stand.

"Officer Shaw," Flatten initiated his questioning with the Captain of the Investigative Division of the Sheriff's office, "In the course of your investigation did you ever go to the home of the defendant, Linda May Burnett?"

"Yes."

"While you were there did you have occasion to examine a Pontiac car owned by the defendant?"

"Yes I did."

"Could you please tell the court the condition of that car?"

"It was very clean. It was clean inside and out."

"Would you say that it was clean just like anybody else's car who uses their car everyday for transportation?"

"No, not at all. Much more than that. It wasn't just clean, it was immaculately clean."

"Could you describe exactly what you mean by immaculately clean?"

"The trunk of the car was recently repainted. The trunk had also been recently recarpeted. It was so clean it was like it had just rolled off the showroom floor."

"What about the interior of the car?"

"It hadn't been recarpeted, but it was also as clean as a whistle. Not a speck of dirt, no trash, nothing. It was thoroughly cleaned a short time before we got there to investigate."

"What about under the car?"

"Same story. There wasn't anything on the underside of the car that would indicate where the car had been. Even the underside had been recently cleaned."

"How clean did it appear, Captain Shaw? Clean like someone had rubbed a rag over it to get rid of dirt and grease?"

"No, clean like it was professionally steamed clean."

"Did Leo Burnett give you any explanation as to why it was so clean inside, outside, and on the underside?"

"He told me he had just had it steamed clean."

"Did you find anything else at the Burnett House that could be linked to this crime?"

"We found some rope that we took as evidence. And we found a couple of shovels."

"Captain Shaw, you were at the gravesite when the bodies were recovered and you saw the rope on the bodies, didn't you?

"Yes."

"Did the rope you found at the Burnett residence match the rope found on the bodies?"

"No. It was a different size. The bodies were bound with three-eights inch rope. The rope we found at the defendant's home was half-inch."

"You also mentioned shovels, Captain. Did you find anything on the shovels to link them to the crime scene?"

"No, nothing."

"Did they appear to just be shovels like anyone might have around their house?"

"Well, yeah, you could say they were normal shovels for gardening and doing yard work, but you couldn't say they were normal in the sense that they were in the same condition as shovels you'd expect to find around a house."

I thought that was an odd question and odd response from Shaw. I grew up on a farm and a shovel around the house is pretty much just a shovel around the house. I could not see where Flatten was taking this line of questioning.

Flatten turned his head to face the jury and asked, "How were they different?"

"It was obvious from the marks and scrapes on them that

they were not new shovels. They had been used many times," Shaw was significantly overweight and whenever he put two sentences together it seemed like a burst of energy for him. With a silent break and audible gasp for air he continued. "But they were clean. They were really clean. Just like the trunk of the car. Clean like they were just bought at a store."

"Or clean like they'd just been steamed cleaned?" Flatten said as he tilted his hand and looked toward the courtroom ceiling.

"Steam cleaning would get them that clean, yes."

"So you did not find anything on them that would link the shovels to the crime scene, such as dirt from the Gilbert Woods area?"

"No."

"Did you find any dirt on them," Flatten said with a look of deep concern on his face, "dirt like you'd normally find on a shovel around the house."

"No." Captain Shaw slowly spoke every word. "There was not any dirt on the shovels. It was like someone had cleaned them with a cotton swab. Even the small creases in the metal had been cleaned out by someone. The connecting seams between the wood and the metal didn't have any traces of soil, grease, or anything in them. Not one speck anywhere."

"Captain Shaw," Flatten spoke "Captain" slowly and paused slightly after saying it to imprint in the juror's minds this was an expert witness on the stands, "was there anything you found at the Burnett house that could be linked to the deaths of the Phillips family?"

"At the Burnett house? No. Nothing."

"Did you find any items that looked as if they had been recently cleaned up by someone?"

"Oh yes, it was evident somebody had definitely been doing some cleaning up a short time before we got there."

"Cleaning up as one would do after one used a shovel or a car? You know, a little water, wash off a little dirt? Maybe sweep out the car?"

"No. They appeared to be cleaned up to remove all traces of everything. Not like you'd normally wash a shovel down or clean dirt out of your car's trunk."

"Thank you Captain Shaw. We pass the witness."

CHAPTER TEN

The Tape

"They have what?!" Ted raised his voice about an octave. He neither could nor would believe what I was saying. I was having trouble grasping it too. The newsroom suddenly got quiet as reporters' antennas were picking up on something and all ears tuned in to our conversation.

"No." Ted assured me. "You don't do that."

"They did it," I repeated.

"Come on. You're joking," Ted said with a 'you're pulling my leg, aren't you' look on his face. "They took her to a hypnotist!? You have got to be making this up. This doesn't happen in real life."

"Hey, nobody has accused Howell and Erwing of lacking legal innovation in the art of how to defend a client." I grinned and laughed as I tried to assure Ted I was not leading him into some kind of elaborate joke to make him look ridiculous. He just wanted to be certain I was telling the truth because it did not take a lawyer to figure out that this was a really obtuse method of defending a client.

The cat was out of the bag. Of all the revelations and eye-popping disclosures during the trial this was the most confounding one that neither I nor any other reporter or lawyer had ever heard. The word leaked to the district attorney's office shortly before the trial began that the highly innovative and cunningly imaginative legal strategists Howell and Erwing took Linda to a hypnotist. I was as flabbergasted as Ted. Everyone was grasping for answers on this one. And everyone was salivating for the details.

It was so preposterous I was still having trouble making Ted believe me, so I started filling in the blanks. "Here's what I've heard. According to my sources at the courthouse, the hypnotist put her into a trance and she went through every little detail of the night of the murders. She had in effect, confessed to a hypnotist. And just to make sure Howell and Erwing had it for safe keeping; a recording of the entire session was made! Can you believe that?"

"Holy shit ... Unbelievable."

"Nothing's unbelievable in this trial or with her attorneys. Legally speaking, Howell and Erwing are redefining the word unbelievable. And redefining dumb and dumber."

Between Joe and Linda they had spun a tale that would not even fit into a country song. There was booze, there was honky-tonkin', there was sex, there was cheating, there was plotting out, and carrying out, mass murder. What Joe did not reveal shooting his mouth off, Howell and Erwing provided. This time, big time. Once again Howell and Erwing had blundered into gift wrapping evidence for the State to use against them and Linda. A confession under hypnosis. My source in the DA's office said it took them about thirty minutes to file a motion to get it in their possession after they learned of its existence. And that was only because they could not find a secretary who could type faster.

I could see Ted was still having trouble believing what he was hearing so I said, "McGrath gave us some comments on camera. Let's go to the video." I tried to let it soak in that I was not kidding because I could see Ted was still skeptical. I pulled the tape out of our field recorder and walked with him to a video machine to let him hear McGrath for himself so he could, number one, believe I was telling the truth, and number two, listen to McGrath's news conference so he could get some, hopefully sensational, statement to use as a promo for the six o'clock news. McGrath usually obliged the media in his news conferences by giving some kind of sensational or defiant statement. And as a side effect, it would drive Carver nuts. It just seemed to be a natural talent McGrath was born with. He had a knack for getting under Carver's skin. And I knew Carver could not bail water as fast as the defense's case was sinking.

"Carver would never let them do anything like that," Ted said with a look of "gotcha" as he tried to find a hole in this highly unlikely scenario.

"Carver didn't. He didn't have anything to do with it," I said. "They made the tape back in the fall before Carver joined them on the defense. Believe me. They really did, actually, pos-i-tive-ly, take her to a hypnotist."

"When did the State find out about it?" Ted said with a glimmer of belief discernable in his voice.

"Apparently sometime early in December, about a month after they took the case," I continued laying out the details to Ted while I waited for the tape in the field machine to eject so I could insert the tape of the McGrath news conference.

At the point when word leaked out about the tapes, the heat of the Texas summer had given way to fall and Texas football which had given way to the anywhere from forty to seventy degree days of winter in Southeast Texas.

It was April of the following year when Linda's trial began. Area farmers were preparing their fields for summer crops and rice farmers were nurturing their tender sprouts in flooded fields around Winnie just like they have done for nearly a hundred years. But when six o'clock rolled around the attention of the farmers and all of Southeast Texas still shifted to the news.

I knew because every time I was in public, with a reporter's notebook in my hand, or a baseball cap on my head in the grocery store, strangers would come up and ask questions about the trial, what I knew, what I knew but could not report, any little bit of insider information they thought they could get out of me to try to make sense of this whole senseless crime. Every day brought new details about the brutal slaying of the five family members. Through all the months, hearings, motions, statements from lawyers, law officers, and media stories, the public still had a limitless capacity for absorbing any new tiny bit of information about the murders. This was not a tiny bit. This was blockbuster. This was almost as shocking as the arrest of Joe and Linda and certainly opened the door for speculation that would turn every person in the area into an amateur lawyer. Starting with Ted.

"Okay, here's my next question. Are they going to be able to use it in court as evidence?" Ted was fishing and hoping for a news promo that would literally throw the viewers into their chairs and glue them to our channel for the six o'clock news.

"McGrath thinks so," I answered. "I don't know what he's got up his sleeve but he thinks there's a legal precedent for him to get it admitted into the record. You'll see him on the tape. He's got his shit-eating grin on and acting pretty cocky about it."

"How in the world did...what did they...why, uh, why did they make a tape of her under hypnosis?" Ted finally got out a question as he tried to sort out all the implications of this incredibly unlikely legal strategy.

"Don't feel like the Lone Ranger on this," I tried to reassure Ted. "Nobody at the court house or in law enforcement sees any of the logic of making a tape. There isn't a lawyer in the courthouse who isn't as shocked as you are. It's the craziest legal tactic anyone has ever heard. You could hear the jaws hitting the floor as the news spread around the courthouse."

"Well it's certainly interesting," Ted said trying to be a little philosophical about something so nonsensical as the idea began to soak in, "I guess you could say it's certainly fodder for legal discussion."

"It's beyond logic," I said shaking my head still trying to wrap my mind around it as well. "When the word about the tape got around the courthouse you could almost hear a giant flushing sound. A giant flushing sound as if something big, oh, say like maybe the defense for a huge murder case, going down the drain. Or as some others described it, the sound of two attorneys' careers going down the old crapper."

"McGrath is as cocky as ever about the case," I continued. "He says he doesn't need the tape to convict her. He says with or without the tape he's sure he can get a conviction. But at this point nobody wants to listen to McGrath; everybody wants to hear what's on the tape."

"I've got it," I said as I felt a grin breaking out on my face. "Maybe that's it; the defense strategy is to have Linda tell the jury, I didn't do it. I was hit-mo-tized."

It was early in the year following the murders that word leaked out about the tapes. Surprisingly the DA's office had been able to keep their existence quiet. The defense had known for quite a while the State had possession of the tapes but they certainly were not going to talk about them. The defense had enough troubles without having to answer media questions about the content of the tapes and their authenticity. In addition to that it was clearly a big embarrassment for the defense for the tapes to come to the public's attention.

"Here's what we know." I said, continuing to debrief Ted to give him details for writing a headline. "The tape was made November fourteenth, five months after the murders. It was recorded in the office of Linda's attorney, Bill Howell. Howell and Erwing contacted Michael Boulch and hired him do the regressive hypnosis session with Linda and, god only knows why, record it. Now I know you think Howell and Erwing are inept, but this goes beyond dumb to bizarre. You won't believe this. As if they couldn't screw it up enough on their own, Boulch is a deputy constable in

Houston. Can you believe that? They went to a law officer to do the hypnosis. Only Howell and Erwing could make such a massive blunder. These guys could screw up a crowbar."

All the time I am talking to Ted and getting the tape cued up my mind was racing in different directions as the adrenalin rush from this newest development combined with the adrenalin of racing to go on the air. This was so big that we could not wait for a news promo. The radio stations were already running with it and we knew the other two TV stations were also busy getting anchor, script, and floor crew ready to go live. We broke into regular programming to try to win the battle of "Who's first" at informing viewers.

McGrath told me he planned to get the tape admitted into evidence by presenting to the court that on the tape were the voices of Boulch; Linda and Erwing. Another pesky problem for the defense was that Erwing may not have legally been an attorney at that point because of his suspension by the state bar association, and another opening for the state to use to their advantage. It was another one of those little legal details that seemed to haunt Howell and Erwing and show up in the most unlikely and embarrassing places.

McGrath and my courthouse sources filled in the details about how he found out about the tape. In yet another strange twist in the case and in the incredibly bad luck that seemed to haunt Howell and Erwing, a friend of a friend, someone totally uninvolved with the case, heard about the tapes. According to McGrath, the chain of friends led to Calise Blanchard. McGrath would not divulge who leaked the information, but since Boulch was a deputy constable and traveled in law enforcement circles, the friend passing the word on to Blanchard was probably a law officer. Once Blanchard heard about the tape he went straight to McGrath and the paper work started flying to subpoena the tapes.

When the trial reached the point where the State began laying the predicate to get the tapes admitted into evidence, as had happened many times during the trial, the jury was escorted from the courtroom. More than once the jury had been absent for days as legal questions and motions were debated for inclusion in the case. This was the biggest battle of the trial. Few people knew what was on the tapes but the grapevine around the courthouse was telling me that they would blow the defense's case out of the water if they were introduced and send their ship straight to the bottom. And Linda to the electric chair.

The battle began with Calise Blanchard taking the stand and testifying that the State obtained the tapes in a lawful manner. Carver, still trying to undo the damage done by Howell and Erwing, did most of the arguing against their introduction into evidence. There was also a strong sense in the courtroom that Howell and Erwing were just trying to stay quiet and put as much distance as possible between them and this incredibly embarrassing legal blunder. By this time even Howell and Erwing had finally figured out that the tape's existence put a stench on the trial that would stick with it no matter what the verdict.

Although I was like every reporter, grasping a lucky charm in one hand and crossing my fingers on the other in hopes the tapes made it into the trial, I must admit I thought Carver did a good job of damage control. He objected to the tape's admissibility on the grounds that it was part of the defense's investigation, so the State had no right to hear it; that their introduction would violate attorney-client relationship privileges; they violated Linda's right to counsel; that they violated the fifth amendment against self incrimination; and that their admission violated the Texas Code of Criminal Procedures and the Texas State Constitution. He also tried to block their admission by contending they were obtained by unlawful search and seizure. Carver argued that the State willfully withheld information from the defense when it obtained the tapes. He additionally petitioned the court not to admit the tapes because a proper predicate had not been established to show the tapes were admissible. But the problem was, with every legal objection raised,

Carver was signaling to everyone how very, very damaging they were to Linda's defense.

Once McGrath had the tapes it was obvious he expected to use them in the trial. He said to get a conviction he intended to "Shoot with every barrel I have." McGrath fired away fighting for their admission, maintaining proper procedures had been followed and that the tapes were obtained in a completely lawful manner from Boulch in early December after a motion for discovery had been duly and properly filed.

Trying another tactic to avoid the tapes entry into evidence Carver filed a motion for a mistrial. In the motion he cited the extensive statements published by the media which had made the trial the only topic of conversation in southeast Texas for nearly ten months. He also based his motion on the contention that the jury had not been sequestered, that there was extensive coverage of Linda's statements in the media, and the news coverage about the polygraph test. He also objected to what he contended was a large number of statements allowed into the record that were about Joe, not Linda.

Carver was just about everything Howell and Erwing were not. They were stocky and overweight. He was slender and looked like a lawyer when he put on a suit. They handled the case like they were all thumbs; Carver was like a surgeon with a scalpel. I must admit, it was engaging theater watching Carver use every legal precedent and argument he could muster to keep the tape out and somehow unscrew this screwed up mess Howell and Erwing had created. Although every reporter personally knew and liked Carver, we squirmed in our seats hoping he would fail and we would get to hear what was on this incredible tape. It was not just me and the rest of the reporters cheering for the admission, as part of his motions to stop this train wreck, Carver pointed out that the public's insatiable demand for details of the trial were drawing standing room only crowds every day. He said the air of a spectacle and widespread publicity every day made it impossible for Linda to get a fair trial in

Jefferson County. He also filed a motion for a continuance in the trial so it could be held at a later time after community emotions calmed down. Delaying a verdict in the case was the last thing any of the reporters, or the public, wanted to happen.

It was difficult, but we did not want to get tossed out of Judge Gist's court, so there were no cheers, only beaming smiles from the reporter's section when the motion for a mistrial was denied. Judge Gist also denied Carver's motion to sequester the jury, and he disallowed the motion for a continuance and ordered the trial continue as scheduled. Like McGrath, Carver "shot with every barrel he had," but not one shot hit its mark.

After the court ruled on those legal objections, with the jury still out of court in the jury room, Judge Gist continued to hear arguments against the tapes admission. The state began their offense with Michael Boulch, the hypnotist who interrogated Linda under hypnosis. He identified Linda as the person in his office with her attorney for the hypnosis session, the person he had hypnotized, and finally, he identified her as the voice on the tape.

Trying desperately to stop the damage from spreading, the defense countered with a string of their expert witnesses to try again to block the tape's admission. First on the stand was David Salmon, a technical expert who testified the recording was made at different times and it was not one continuous session because of different audio levels and background sounds. Salmon went so far as to say that in his opinion the tape was altered. According to him, the tape had almost eight and a half minutes erased, was recorded at different times, and even had portions dubbed in, as if to imply someone had taken the tape and erased some of the story and recorded over the erasure with more incriminating information.

It is standard procedure in trials and I had seen it several times before. One side presents an expert saying one thing and the other side then comes back with an expert saying the exact opposite. It began with the State putting their experts on the stand who said it was a virgin tape used for the recording. The State also put on

Walter Rotsch, an investigator from Port Neches to testify that Salmon, the defense's expert on tapes was a dog trainer and private investigator, not the audio expert he claimed to be. He also testified Salmon had a reputation for dishonesty in Southeast Texas.

The defense countered with two law officers and a Harris County grand jury assistant foreman who testified Salmon had an excellent reputation for honesty and integrity. Punch-counterpunch-counterpunch. From my perspective it looked like the State's punches were having the most impact.

Next Linda took the stand to say the conversation between her and Boulch was not what it appeared. She said the tape was a medium of communication but not made under hypnosis. When questioned about the tape she said she could not recall what they had discussed. When asked if it was her voice on the tape, she took the Fifth Amendment.

At that point the state asked the court to force Linda to give them a voice exemplar to ascertain the probability that the voice on the tape was hers. That was one of the major battles her defense team successfully fought. She never gave a voice exemplar as Carver effectively protected her with the Fifth Amendment rights against self-incrimination. Finally, a victory for the defense.

Erwing was also called to the witness stand. He testified the defense made the tape as a medium of communication but he never listened to it after he left Boulch's office. He admitted he read transcripts of the tape or listened to a copy of the district attorney's tape but never heard the defense's tape. Erwing said he was not present the entire time the tape was being recorded. He said the tape appeared, in his terminology, "to be the same subject, matter-wise," but not in the same order as he remembered. By the time he finished with his testimony people in the courtroom, including reporters, were shaking their heads trying to follow his convoluted logic. It sounded like intended vagueness and you could hear the sound of more water rushing into the defense's sinking boat.

Following Erwing, Boulch took the stand again. Trying to

make sense of Howell and Erwing's logic, he said they told him they wanted to make the tape to find out if anybody had seen Joe and Linda that night. They wondered if there were any witnesses she might be able to remember by going back over the night under hypnosis. Boulch also testified that Howell and Erwing told him part of their motivation to make the tape was to have an ace up their sleeve if Linda wanted to get retribution from her attorneys if the trial did not turn out to her satisfaction.

At that point heads were shaking, audible moans and gasps from people in the courtroom, and muffled snickers from the reporters' area. We knew we were all formulating the headlines in our minds. I could hear our anchor's voice in my head blaring out the promo, "Idiots make blackmail tape! Linda confesses all! Details at six!"

To make matters even worse Boulch raised more questions about Howell and Erwing's legal expertise and intentions when he testified they confided in him there was big money to be made from what Linda could remember about the night of the murders. Boulch said both Howell and Erwing told him there was big money to be made from a book about the murders or from selling the story to a detective magazine.

At that point I wondered if they would give her pastor a cut of the sales since he had recommended she fire her original attorney and hire this dynamic defense duo. I felt certain that every night before McGrath went to bed he thanked God for the trio of Linda's pastor, Howell and Erwing. A perfect crime was undone by a perfect group of screw ups.

Carver fired back salvos doing his best at damage control. He tried to make it appear this was all some kind of plot by the district attorney's office. When he asked Boulch why he was testifying Boulch calmly said the only reason was because he was subpoenaed and he did not want to go to jail. Boulch said that on his part he did not breech any confidentiality by divulging to anyone the contents of the tape.

Then we all got to witness a rare spectacle. Flatten, the Assistant District Attorney, called McGrath, the District Attorney, and who had been in court for every second of the trial, to the stand to testify that Howell had told him more than once the tape was to be used for a book. Given Howell's inclination to take events with an air of joviality, it was very plausible he may have jokingly said that to McGrath. But given Howell's profession as a lawyer and in the middle of a trial, he would also be familiar with the legal phrase given everyone in their first introduction to the criminal justice system that "any statements made can and will be used against you." He would certainly have known that if given the opportunity, McGrath would take a statement like that and beat the hell out of him with it in court.

The defense followed by calling Howell who contradicted McGrath. Howell denied all accusations about making the tape to sell the story or making the tape to use for blackmail if Linda wanted retribution. Facing the media outside the court he stuck to his story that he had never made any such a statement to McGrath.

In addition to making the tape, Howell and Erwing followed that mistake with more critical errors. The State argued that Boulch was not at any point Linda's attorney; therefore the attorney-client relationship had been breached from the beginning. The State brought out other witnesses to testify that the tape was transcribed, handled, and listened to by more than one secretary in Boulch's office and also in Howell and Erwing's. The State showed that the tape went through so many non-attorney hands during its creation and transcriptions that the defense had totally and thoroughly demolished any attorney-client privileges.

With the jury box still empty, the State and defense argued legal precedent vs. legal precedent over the admissibility of the tape as Judge Gist listened. The defense knew it was a life or death argument. The State felt the same way. Everything hung on the admission of the tape.

"No case like this exists, your honor," Flatten addressed the court. "Never before has the side not making the tape put the tape into evidence."

"During the Watergate trials would Judge Sirica have not allowed the Butterfield tapes into evidence because of the eighteen minute gap?" Flatten answered the defense's accusations about the possibility of erasures on the tape.

Carver came back even more adamant that the tapes be withheld from evidence. "This is neither the time nor the place to make new law," Carver implored judge Gist. "A human life is at stake."

It was new legal territory. There was nothing in the books as a precedent. Judge Gist knew that. He had been a lawyer and judge in Jefferson County for more than a decade and he was also aware that he did not want to spend a lot of the county's money only to have the case overturned. In addition, he definitely did not want a higher appellate court telling him he made the wrong decision in allowing the tape into evidence. However, he was also known as a judge who was willing to try new approaches if it made the system work more efficiently in reducing the court's tremendous workload, while still assuring justice for the defendant.

Carver's first objection to the tape's admission was based on the grounds that the tape was protected by the attorney-client relationship. Judge Gist overruled. On his second objection that the proper predicate had not been laid out for the tape's admission Judge Gist also overruled.

Overruled once, twice. These were two critical issues and the defense lost both times. It was now a worst case scenario for the defense. Consulting with Linda outside of the courtroom, Carver, Howell and Erwing began preparing her for the likelihood that the case was no longer winnable.

Carver gave it his best shot. He researched everywhere and did everything he could to keep the tapes out. Unfortunately for Linda he had joined the defense after the tape was made and all he could do was attempt to throw up some roadblocks, create some diversions, and try to tidy up some of the damage done when the State got possession of the tapes. For quite some time it was evident from the attitudes of McGrath and Carver that the tapes were not only incriminating but devastating to the defense. With their admission McGrath was holding nothing but aces in his hands, dealt him courtesy of Howell and Erwing.

It was 2:30 in the afternoon when the judge made his ruling. For the first time in a week the jury came back into the courtroom to continue the trial. Anticipation in the media and spectators was at the highest level since the trial began.

The tape would be admitted into evidence. The State had what it wanted. I had what I wanted. I looked down the row of reporters and there was nothing but smiles and a couple of "thumbs up" discretely given where only the other reporters could see. Glancing quickly to the defense table I saw a collective look of doom descend over Linda and her defense team. There was no mistaking the message on their faces that the subject matter on the tapes was catastrophic to their case.

On the other side Flatten and McGrath were grinning from ear to ear. Reporters and headline writers were giddy with delight. It was great drama, it was great courtroom theatrics, and for Southeast Texas, it was the greatest show on earth.

CHAPTER ELEVEN

The State Plays the Tape

In all the hundreds of hours I had spent in courtrooms there was nothing in any way comparable to this. I had heard horrific details of horrid crimes, but never from the lips of the accused. Not only was this great theater, it was also historic ground. This would be the first time a confession under hypnosis had ever been made and then admitted into evidence for the whole world to hear. As a student at American University in Washington D.C. I got to sit in the Supreme Court for about an hour listening to history being decided. This trial was also historic, and there was already speculation that the case could go all the way to the Supreme Court. Maybe I would be back in the Supreme Court again, but this time as a reporter. So many options and scenarios were running through my head that it was hard to keep track of the basic details of my job, such as getting the bombshell information on the tapes back to the station so it could explode on the air. All 3 stations had cameras and cables strung all over the hallway and connected to transmitter trucks parked outside and microwaving a signal back to the station. I was ready, my photographer was ready, the signal was beaming back to the station and the director was in the control room waiting for the signal to break into network programming and go live. Not only was the media all set, TV sets and radios all over Southeast Texas that were normally off were turned on in anticipation of hearing what was on the tape.

Just like every other day of the trial the courtroom was packed and this day there were people who could not get in standing in the hall and peering in through the small window in the door. There was one difference this day. More deputies, badges, and guns were in the courtroom than I had ever seen for any trial.

I was in awe of Judge Gist's Court every time I entered it. I love architecture, especially old buildings that belong to another era. The scene reminded me of the big courtroom in the movie *To Kill a Mocking Bird*. All that was lacking was a filled gallery of people craning their necks as they looked down on the main floor of distinguished looking southerners, the men with their coats off and fanning themselves with their straw hats, and the genteel women ever so elegantly and gently unfolding their collapsible fans to give themselves some relief from the heat. To complete the picture all that was needed was Gregory Peck standing in his summertime suit to address the jury, and huge ceiling fans making a faint whirring noise above.

It also gave Linda's trial an air of grand theater. This was the most compelling legal event to ever take place in that court, the county, and the region. This was a courtroom full of people almost breathless to assure not one word or inflection to each word escaped their ears. This was the only mass murder trial ever heard in Jefferson County, one of the most heinous crimes ever committed in Southeast Texas, and it was definitely one of the strangest defense strategies ever used in any case. Everyone knew this was a precedent-setting trial and a trial that had grown larger than life and was assured to live forever in local history. I knew I had the lead story and every person listening at exactly six o'clock would be totally focused on every word coming out of my mouth. I felt the excitement pumping through my veins. It was history and as a reporter I had a reserved front row seat.

There was one very distinct difference in the courtroom that day. Two loudspeakers about 18 inches wide and two feet tall were perched on top of five foot stands. As if to accentuate the importance of the tapes, and to assure everyone heard the voice on the tape lay out the details of the crime, the district attorney's office had made sure to accommodate everyone in the court with special loud speakers set up so that everyone heard everything on the tape. The stage was set. The audience anxiously awaited the curtain to rise. The reporters were all in their places. Every one of us had extra pens and notepads as backup to make sure we did not miss anything.

I scanned the courtroom as I did every day. Counting Linda's husband Leo, there were probably less than a half dozen people in the courtroom I could identify as sympathetic to her. Her daughters had been in court for some portions of the trial but they were not there that day. The rest of the audience was there to hear the proof of what they already believed about Linda's participation in the murders. For the crowd the defining moment of the trial had finally arrived even though Linda never admitted the voice on the tape was hers. As far as the people in the courtroom were concerned, until that point the trial had all been preliminary jousting by attorneys. This was the bottom line, where the truth trumps the lie.

For the news media there was ten months of hashing and rehashing the slowly surfacing details of the crime. This was it. Every TV set in the area would be tuned to the six o'clock news that night. Every newspaper in every vending rack would be sold.

The tape player was ready. The speakers were tested and worked perfectly. But in addition to the tape, to make sure all the quotes were correct, the court and DA's office generously accommodated every reporter with a transcript of the tape.

With all the equipment and all the actors and participants in place, Judge Gist ordered the tape played. Every person in the courtroom went into a trance as the button was pushed and the tape began. For the next hour the entire audience sat, hypnotized by the voice coming out of the speakers.

Flatten and McGrath confidently leaned back in their large wooden chairs to get comfortable for the hour long tape. Carver and Howell took note pads and pens to write down any thought or weakness they could glean from the tape and use as a defense. As the hissing sound of the tape filled the courtroom, the recording began with the tick-tock rhythm of a metronome. Linda appeared nervous and put her fingers in her ears. Next was the voice of Michael Boulch initiating a hypnotic trance. The next sound was the voice of a woman. I began following her words with my verbatim copy of the transcript. The transcript began with:

A.   I cannot let anybody oppress me again, because if I do, even if you were now to try to get me to do something, and I didn't feel it was right, I mustn't let you talk me into it. Not ever again. When Leo tries to talk me into things, I mustn't let him confuse me, because he tries terribly to confuse me and to make me think like he thinks, either, you know--

Q.   Go on your own judgment?

A.   I really have to because see, I really wanted to let these people live and to kill him. I really wanted that, and I feel like kicking my own tail because I didn't do it that way. I really am guilty about that.

Q.   When did you first know that you were gonna be going out there to commit the murders?

A.   When I said to myself that he's really gonna do it?

Q.   When he said we're going out, when was the plan actually---

A.   We went out Friday night and made all the routine things, we went out and we went around the house and we was gonna do it, and I don't know why we did not, I don't remember why we didn't, something wasn't, uh, he got cold feet I believe.

Q. This was in July?

A. June. June thirtieth.

Q. Were they in the house?

A. Yeah. We had dug the grave, but I don't know why we didn't go. I don't remember. And then, cause they were there. Oh!, we was waiting for the couple and the boy to leave, the young couple, to leave. We was hoping they would go on, but we knew that this had got to be done this weekend, because if we didn't do it this weekend, it couldn't be done.

Q. Why were you going to do it? What was the purpose?

A. I don't know. He didn't really want -- maybe it was an ego builder for him.

Q. Well, I mean was there money, or insurance ---?

A. No, no, no, no, -- no, no. Uh, he wanted to find out where his ex-wife was, where his ex-in-laws, this was his ex-in-laws. He wanted his children back is all he ever wanted. I don't think he ever really wanted Mary back, he wanted his kids back. And, uh, I think he did it for kicks, if you want to know what I think.

Q. Had he had --?

A. It was a fantasy of his, I think.

Q. Had he had any conflicts with them before, fights with the man -- ?

A. Oh, yes, yes.

Q. Well did he lose -- ?

A. I think he did always lose. And he wanted to win. Mentally, this is what I assume now. He wanted to win and he used me to win.

Q. So he took you out there. All right. What day did this occur, the actual -- ?

A. The routine run?

Q. The routine run was June thirtieth?

A. Right.

Q   Then when you went out to actually do it?

A.   Saturday, July first.

Q.   What time did you get out there?

A.   After dark, nine o'clock.

Q.   Were they up?

A.   Yeah.

Q.   Just in your own words, then, the best that you can remember; where did you leave from to go out there? Where were you at, you and Joe?

A.   We were at his house and we went to Rodair and parked his car and got in mine, and we went on out there in my car. Parked my car on the road. We walked through, we crawled through the weeds, uh, close to the fence row, up towards away from Interstate ten, there's an open field, a rice field, with high weeds on the side of the road. We crawled through the weeds, got to the edge of the property, went on up through the property, I think I fell over a swing set, real bright, noise, and it didn't bother them at all. We walked around that front yard and just watched the, watched them and watched them, and I thought to myself, anybody outside my house, around my yard, and I'm gonna know who's there. I cannot understand how they did not realize we were there.

Q.   What kind of a weapon did you have? Did you have more than one weapon?

A.   Yes, Uh, I had a rifle, a twenty-two caliber rifle, fifteen shot. Automatic. Uh, I don't believe I took the knife that time, because I was afraid of losing it. I may have had a twenty-two Ruger --

Q.   Automatic, or --?

A.   Automatic.

Q.   Did Joe have a weapon?

A.   It's not automatic; it's the kind that shells go in the bottom.

Q.   Okay. That's an automatic.

A.   Oh, it wasn't the revolving type. He had the same type of gun but it was a forty-five.

Q.   Forty-five automatic?

A.   Yeah, he had, uh, mace --

Q.   Mace?

A.   Yeah. Spray. Never used it. Uh, he had the handcuffs, I had the rope. I might have had the tape too, I don't know.

Q.   Where did you get the rope and the tape, the handcuffs and the gun?

A.   Uh, the guns were his. The tape, I bought the tape somewheres. Uh, --

Q.   Department store, or --

A.   In a Woolco's, I think it was Woolco's, could have been Walgreen's. The rope, I bought at Guzardo's Feed on Twin City Highway. I told the man when I bought the rope that it was for a swing up at my daddy's.

Q.   For a swing?

A.   Uh huh. For the kids.

Q.   What's the man's name that you bought it from?

A.   Fred Guzardo. He doesn't remember. Uh, he thinks I had all my kids in there the day that I bought the rope. I did not have anybody with me the day I bought the rope. But he thinks I had all the kids with me. He doesn't really remember. He's just making it up, you know, it sounds good so say it.

Fred Guzardo. Incredible. I could not believe it. No wonder McGrath called him to the stand. Linda's attorneys made the tape and Linda very conveniently made the list of witnesses for the D.A. to contact and call to the witness stand. I kept my professional face on in court, but later I could not help but laugh at what a fiasco Howell and Erwing had created. How could they screw this up any worse?

Q.   Oh, okay. Did you have any feelings at that time, like you shouldn't be doing it or you should do it, or you might be caught or any emotion at all while you were planning it.

A.   It was exciting and fun. It was doing something besides sitting home; washing dishes, making the bed and listening to Leo raise hell!

Q.   Had you ever thought about killing Leo?

A.   Probably, but never really do it, I don't think.

Q.   Did Joe ever bring up that, about killing your husband?

A.   Yes. Yes, for money. I didn't realize how much Leo was worth, accidentally dead, he's worth $180,000, accidentally dead. But see, that's Wendy's father, and he has been good to me. Sexually perfect, couldn't be any better. Uh, first man in my life that I have truly found compatible sexually, if we could work out the thing about him leaving my kids alone, fine. I'd go to the end of the earth with him. But, not the way he's going.

Q.   You think he's sexually attracted to the older one?

A.   Yes, I think that, uh, his first wife, is the reason I think this. She said he was sadistic by nature, and this is why she left him, over their daughter, who is now twenty-one. Leo's fifty-three. And he takes care of himself. He looks to be about forty.

My eyes immediately darted to Leo, who was listening with his head bowed. His glasses were off and his eyes closed as the tape went into their intimate family relationships. While he was suffering the pains of what was being amplified to every person in the courtroom and would later be amplified through every news media in the area, Linda also had her head down, but she had her glasses on and was reading along with the transcript. Some of the people were staring at Linda with disbelief at what they were hearing, some staring with contempt for her burning in their eyes as it was becoming more and more evident she was there when the Phillips family was murdered.

Q.   Okay, so you were crawling through -- you were out in the front yard looking in. What happened from there?

A.   We walked around the house. There was a car come up, I

guess it was Saturday night, I don't know, I've got the two of them confused. Uh, we went out on the other side of the house in the pasture sitting waiting for the persons to leave. We come back, walked around, the front door. Joe started cutting the screen. I went in first.

Q. Where did you go in, through the back?

A. Into a front room. The house is laid out like this, more like this.

Q. So when you walked into the door first --

A. You walked across in this, this bedroom through this bedroom where they had their luggage, and some stuff, and the little boy was playing ball in the next room. I don't remember what I did. I, uh, think that, uh, I think that I had the child in my hand, I'm not too sure. The child was back and forth, and it was used as a threat.

Q. So what did Joe say? Did he walk in and hold the gun -- ?

A. He had the baby.

Q. He had the baby?

A. I think.

Q. Did you walk in and hold the weapon on the people?

A. Uh huh. Yeah.

Q. What did you tell them, not to move or -- ?

A. Uh huh.

Q. Did you say anything like you were going to kill them or anything like that?

A. No. Said we had some questions to ask. Uh, the only statement I believe that I made was that Mary had cheated us out of some money. She had stolen some money. It was a diversion, trying to get the girl's attention, because she was getting restless and I wanted to control her mentally by conversation, not by force. I didn't like the force part. Uh, Joe was hassling at the old man. The old man became hostile and ran through, to the kitchen, and Joe cramped him in the head with a forty-five. Uh, I don't know, there was mass confusion about this time. I don't remember too much about what was going on. Uh, the boy put the handcuffs on the old man. The girl tied up the old lady with the rope. Joe tried to get me to put the handcuffs on somebody and I couldn't do it, I bumfuzzled that. I got upset, maybe nervous, frightened. I don't know what I got, and then I became mean. I became, I felt mean. He talked and I assisted him in talking about if you want to live, you better do what you're told to do, things of this nature, the pattern of this conversation. The boy was very intelligent, intelligent enough to control the other members of the family, and so was the young girl, the woman, she was, maybe thirty-two, I'm not sure how --

Q.   His wife?

A.   Yes, and, uh, I convinced them that they wouldn't be hurt if they behaved themselves. See, the guilt really is mine, not Joe's. Joe's crazy. I was crazy for going along with it, but I was more vicious than he was, because I had the ability to convince these people that they would be perfectly all right.

Q.   Did you know at that time you were going to kill them.

A.   No, I thought he was gonna do it.

Good Grief. Even the hypnotist was against her. I was not hearing one word that was sympathetic to Linda or might help her cause. It was obvious Boulch was aware before the session ever started that his job was to hypnotize a murderer and get all the details of that murder. Nowhere was there even the faintest hint that he was trying to gather information to exonerate her from the crime or place her somewhere else to give her an alibi. Boulch was as relentless in his hypnotic interrogation as McGrath was for the State. There was no doubt in his voice as he questioned her. It was obvious they were talking about a real event, not a story concocted under hypnosis. And a story of such minute detail that it was never intended to have ever been heard by anyone other than Linda's attorneys.

Q.   Well, you knew that you were going to kill them.

126

A.   Well, we knew that if we walked in there and they recognized us we couldn't walk off and let 'em live, now could we, because they would identify us and we would get in all kinds of trouble. That was -- and he really wanted to kill that old man and old woman. The boy, the girl and the baby, if they had of left they wouldn't have been killed. If they had of just gone about their business, they was, you know, I read in the papers afterwards, they had gone to a friend's house to eat supper and stuff, so they should have stayed there, because they wouldn't have been involved if they would have stayed away. Because we tried to eliminate anyone being involved in there, in this, except the old man and the old woman.

Q.   You could have waited until later, couldn't you, until they would have left?

A.   We did wait, they didn't leave.

Q.   What time was it approximately, that you broke -- ?

A.   After bout eleven. Because we waited outside all this time. The uh, the night before we had waited and we knew, I don't know, if he impressed on my mind or if I impressed on his mind, I really don't remember, that it had, he had to work, had to go back to work, and not only that, the shots would have been heard at any other time and people would have been suspicious of shots, but on the fourth of July, no one would be suspicious. I mean, that was our reasoning, the logic that we used.

Q.   Okay, now that was the first of July?

A.   July first, the weekend. Down there firecrackers go off the whole weekend, specially, anytime it falls on a weekend, like Friday through the fourth, everything's wild down there, kind of exciting. So we knew this would be the time to do anything we wanted to do. The next time to be able to do anything would be on Halloween, or on Labor Day, and he did not want to wait that long to do anything about this.

Q. Okay, so you convinced the people that they weren't going to be hurt?

A. Right.

Q. Then what happened after that?

A. We took them and put 'em in the car.

Q. Put 'em in the car?

A. Put 'em in the boy's car. Took them to the grave that we had pre-dug. I drove my car, he drove that car, I followed him. He had all the people in the back seat. No, he had the boy, the old man and the old lady in the back seat, which was quite a load, those big people, and the little boy and the woman was in the front seat. I still wonder how he controlled all of them. I really don't know. We went on to the, where the site where the grave was. I parked my car on the road; he drove the car that he was in into a pasture, got them out of the car, left the baby in the car, lined them up and made them kneel down on the ground behind the car. It was dark; there wasn't any moon out at all. He had a fluorescent light, red light, flash light, service issue, and we taped their mouths. During this time, I talked to them constantly to keep 'em calmed down, telling the, you know, just to play along with him, and that I would kill him and at that time I didn't really think that I was, but then it imbedded within my mind that that's what I should do. Well, I waited too long about doing it, that's the only problem. I waited too long. He mixed up, he had a solution mixed up, that he injected with a hypodermic needle into their arms, necks, wherever, I don't even know where he injected them, cause I wouldn't look cause I don't like to see people get shots. It was buggin' me, you know, I didn't like to see the skin being broken. It bothered me. Then I turned my back and I don't know what he did. The mosquitoes were eating on them and I asked him to keep the mosquitoes off of the, because within my mind at this point, I wanted to kill him but I didn't know how to do it.

Incredulous. The voice I am hearing on the recorder may have been under hypnosis, but the voice coming out of the woman was as unemotional as if she were reading a grocery list. For several minutes she had just intricately described a crime scene and her role in leading five persons to their death. If there was any remorse, it did not come through on the tape.

Q.   What did he put into it, what did he inject? Something to kill them?

A.   Yes. Yes. He told me that it would kill them. And in my mind, that's the reason I went ahead and went along with him because I couldn't figure out how I was going to get everything straightened out. You know, it had gotten to such a mess at this point, how could I get out of this. If I killed him, what would I do, cause there they were. He had already given them this shot, I felt like they would probably die for sure. And I needed him to get me everything squared away you know, to get that car out of there and, uh, everything. But I really wanted several times to blow his head off, and I wished I had of.

When those words came out of the speakers I looked around the courtroom to see how that scenario was playing out. I know I had disgust and disbelief covering my entire face. And I was right about the audience. I could see the same look in dozens of faces in the courtroom. Written on faces all over the stunned audience was the question, *"They injected them with roach poison? It was not enough to kill them? They had to make them suffer incredible pain and torture as well? How could one human do something so sadistic to another?"* I turned my eyes back to my copy of the transcript and kept making notes.

Q.   Okay. What happened after that, after they were behind the car and kneeling down?

A.   Well, we took 'em to the gravesite, that's where he injected them, at the grave site, and then, he walked them into the grave.

Q.   How deep was the grave?

A.   I think about, it must have been, about five foot deep.

The pictures began playing in my mind. My thoughts went back to that morning the previous July when I went to the grave to get video. Rain had filled it in a little. I could see the hole, about four feet deep, some scraps of crime scene tape laying around, and the eerie feeling that this was a scene where events would not die, would not stay buried, but would linger around that disgusting hole forever. Quickly my mind snapped back when the hypnotist started asking about the five victims who at one point all stood around the grave. It was the same hole I saw. It was the same ground I stood on. It was an image I will always have in my mind.

Q.   They weren't struggling or trying to do anything?

A.   No, the damn fools just got into the grave. I talked them into the grave. I talked 'em into it. I convinced them that I would that, you know, that I would shoot them in the arm or leg or something. And in my mind, I wanted to do this, but then I knew I'd better not, cause Joe would kill me. And I was very confused, very confused. I didn't know what I, what to do. And he put the gun, I handed him the gun, for him to shoot them, I believe, and then he handed the gun back to me and said something about, "We're in this -- we're in this together." And I believe I shot all four of them, I don't know, I really don't know.

Q.   You don't remember shooting them?

A.   Yeah, I remember shooting them and I remember the blood flowing from their bodies, from their heads. But I, it was something that uh, I really don't know; I think I blocked it out cause I don't want to think about it. I don't know who was shot first, whether it was the old woman or the old man. And then the other two were put in there, under the illusion that they were only winged, the other two in the grave were only winged or something. And then Joe wanted me, I don't remember how he went about going back to get the baby or anything, but I told him, "No way!", that he'd have to do it, I wouldn't do it. I would not do it. And I told him, I said, "You're talking about," I believe this is what I said, "Talking about being in it fifty-fifty, and that's why I think I killed the other four people and he killed the baby, cause I told him, I said, "You're killin' the baby 'cause I'm not killin' the baby." I think I told him, "If the baby's going to be killed, you're killin' the baby; I'm not killin' the baby." And, because he said we were involved in it fifty-fifty, if one of us got caught, both of us were caught. We took some cord after we got 'em in the grave and everybody was, I turned my back when he shot the baby; I did not let myself look at the baby. That was too much. I asked him, I believe I asked him or wanted to ask him, one way or the other, to let's take the baby and leave the baby somewheres. And now I'll either agree that we would probably get caught if we had of done that, we would probably gotten caught anyway. This crime was perfect if he hadn't opened his mouth!

Every reporter was scanning the courtroom for reaction. We just heard a very cold and calculating woman talk about killing four people with no remorse or hesitation whatsoever, but was just too much of a good mother to kill a 3-year-old child. Her only remorse was that Joe had opened his mouth and ruined a perfect crime. There were women audibly crying. There were men shaken, and on the verge of tears. There were a lot of tears from the Phillips' section of the courtroom. Handkerchiefs and tissues were visible all over the crowd. My head was whirling trying to capture all of the rage, hatred, repulsion, and gut-wrenching emotion engulfing the courtroom while trying to fix my mind on what my story would be, what would be my lead, could the tape contain anything more dramatic than what we just heard? I could see faces of people in the crowd who were ready to take her outside and hang her right then. Texas justice, she had her fair trial. Now hang her. I had never heard or seen a crowd so moved by testimony. I was not the only one. You could see the tenseness in the faces of the bailiffs as well. They had their hands on their guns and a look of real concern that a riot could break out in the courtroom. Even Judge Gist appeared a little apprehensive about the situation.

Q.   What did you do with the weapons?

A.   Joe tended to the weapons. He destroyed the rifle, strung it all over the highway. And I do not have any positive thought on what happened to the rifle. There was only one gun; it was a rifle, twenty-two caliber automatic rifle.

Q.   The two pistols weren't used?

A.   Only to hit the old man in the head.

Q.   Did Joe keep the forty-five that he hit him in the head with?

A.   I don't know. I don't know what he did with the guns.

Q.   How about the syringe?

A.   We threw it off the bridge. Either threw it off the bridge or we threw it in the grass, up and down the side of the highway. I don't -- I'm not too sure. We disposed of everything.

I disposed of the rope. I put it in a convenient spot where people would pick it up, and they did, at a fishing spot between Nederland and Port Acres. In the weeds. It rained and the, during that time it rained and the rope must have looked old, and someone said, "Well, you know, this fell off the car or something," what I suspected.

Q.   Who covered the grave up after the -- ?

A.   We did.

Q.   Both of you?

A.   Yes.

Q.   You had the shovels with you?

A.   Right. My shovels.

Q.   They were in the trunk of your car?

A.   Yes.

Q.   How far away was the grave from the car?

A.   Fifty feet or more. Walking distance easy, running distance.

Again my mind jerked quickly back to the grave. Her description was right on accurate. It was uncanny. They did pick the perfect spot. The grave was just a short distance from the road which made it easy to walk the Phillips to it, but it was in the middle of trees and thick underbrush that made it perfectly invisible to anyone driving by. It was not even seen by passersby when the dirt was piled up high on the ground around the hole, waiting for the rendezvous with the Phillips, Joe, and Linda.

Q.   Did you leave the grave dirt on top, or did you put weeds and things on top?

A.   Camouflaged it very good, stomped the grave down where it wouldn't sink later on, where there wouldn't be any, you could walk over it. Even the Sheriff's department said they would have walked over it and walked over it and never found them.

Q.   How did they find them?

A.   Joe took 'em out there to it.

Q.   He took them right to it?

A.   Right.

Q.   Did Joe ever tell you that he had murdered anyone else? Before that?

A.   He said he was involved with some illegal things.

Q.   But you, yourself had never -- ?

A.   No, not in that aspect, no.

Q.   Just a housewife?

A.   More or less. Uh, I like to steal. I think it's a great ambition of mine to steal.

Q.   Shoplifting?

A.   Yes. Not because I've ever wanted anything. It's because it's fun. That's the only thing I can think of that I've ever done. And it was for fun. I got a neurotic kick out of outsmarting somebody. You know, be standing there talking to a Security Guard and walk off with something. That kind of stuff. Uh, that's the only kind of crime that I've ever committed. That was knowingly in my mind at this time a crime.

It was gallows humor, but there were a few snickers in the courtroom and from the reporter's section. *All she ever wanted to be was a shoplifter? Amazing. She had no aspirations for major crime. How endearing.*

It did not play very well right after her unemotionally retelling how she killed four adults and watched the blood run out of the their bodies, executed with a single gunshot to the back of the head, just like the pros do.

Q.	What did you all do after you disposed of everything? Where did you go? Where was your husband?

A.	He was at home.

Q.	Was he concerned? Didn't he ask where you were at?

A.	He knew where I was at.

Q.	He knew you were out there killing those people?

A.	Yes. He didn't know why. I had given him a fictitious reason which I really don't care to go into.

Q.	I promise.

A.	Okay. I, uh, I really don't want to be asked, cause I'd rather not say the truth about that.

Q.	It's up to you.

A.	Not that part; I'd rather you not ask me. Uh, --
	I was scribbling notes as fast as I could but at that point my pen stopped and my head popped up from my notepad. *What? Do not stop there. Let us know everything. You have just confessed to murdering four people and being an accessory to the murder of a fifth. Why hold anything back now?*

Q.	Did anyone else besides your husband know?

A.	Just Joe.

Q.	What did your husband say when you told him? That's not something that you go home every day and tell your husband that you're gonna go kill somebody, or several people. He must have had some reaction to it.

Once again all the eyes in the courtroom shifted to Linda's husband Leo. As he had through most of the tape, he was sitting there with his head down, hiding both his face and his emotions. At this point he was very aware that with any sign of emotion he would be reading about it and hearing about it in every newspaper article, radio, and TV story that day.

A.   He didn't really care.

Q.   Didn't care?

A.   How we did it.

Q.   You think he believed you?

A.   No. No, not really.

Q.   Did you tell him who you were going with?

A.   Yes.

Q.   Wasn't he, if he's jealous, wasn't he a little concerned?

A.   But, I pacified his mind with another answer, a fictitious answer, okay? That would be another lifetime explanation.

Q.   No problem. I was just curious more or less on, I thought why, if he knew why he wasn't concerned about your being with Joe but --

A.   He was satisfied with a reasonable answer. Even at this time, he doesn't really realize that, uh, Joe, and I were sexually, you know, partners as well as partners in murder, he doesn't realize that...maybe he realizes it, but he doesn't want to accept it. That was the only man that I have fooled around on, well, that I have fooled around with since I've been married to Leo.

Q.   Do you think that, uh -- ?

A.   And this was because of the feeling of, I think what started it is when Leo started wanting a divorce. I uh, depended on Leo complete.

Q.   Do you think Leo is afraid of you, now that he knows -- ?

A.   No. No. He's more sadistic than I am. By far. No, he's not afraid of me. He'd knock my head off in two seconds if he thought he could get by with it if I wouldn't oppose him. He would want to be brutal if he could get by with it.

Q. Well, he must know that you could pick up a gun, and --

A. Not at this time, he knows he's got me over a barrel. He's been a little bit on the pushy side, because he knows I don't dare do anything to him. That's not saying I don't want to. I don't want to kill him or nothing like that, I just think I'd like to take that belt and make him eat it. I really got a thing about, I, uh, the kids being whupped with a belt, it really makes me mad. No, I don't like it.

At that point I had to bury my head and bite my tongue to keep from laughing. *What a tender heart. Pull the trigger eight times, shooting them in the head and through the eye, then watch the blood oozing out of the bodies is no problem? But your kid being hit with a belt is too much to bear? And don't you know that belt made quite a red mark?*

What a truly odd value system. What a contradictory personality.

Q. Okay, so you disposed of everything. You, did you go straight home in your car?

A. I don't remember. No I didn't go straight home. Of course, after we ditched the other car, which we had to do, the Phillips's car, the young boy's car, uh --

Q. Did you burn it?

A. No, I didn't burn it. Joe come back later and burned it. We wiped all the fingerprints off of it and dumped it and we got in the car, we disposed of all bloody items, the pillow case that was bloody, took it to a, uh, Taylor's Bayou --

Q. What was the pillow case used for?

A. The old man had it up against his head because he was bleeding. I had asked Joe to let him have it. Went back to the house, and cleaned up the house a little bit after all this was over, after we dumped the car.

Q. Did you and Joe drink or eat anything while you were there?

A.   No.

Q.   During that night, I'd like to ask you a personal question. Any questions I ask you you don't have to answer.

A.   I'll answer it. I had sex with him before we went out at my request. Yes.

Q.   Afterwards, you didn't?

A.   No, afterwards, I mean, before, it was just a mental relaxation for me. Because we had some time to kill, why not? He looked good, why not?

Q.   Did someone ask you this question before me?

A.   Yeah, and I give 'em a hundred different answers. Anything I choose to tell 'em. If a man's around, sex is just like food. If it's there, enjoy it, if it's not, fine. I don't think a person should just depend on, on communication through sex with another person. I think sex should be just like food, or fishing or anything else. I think it should be for fun. And if it's not, why fool with it. I mean, you're wasting your time and everybody else's time and nobody's gonna get any enjoyment out of it. I mean, that's pretty bold, but uh, --

Q.   The reason I asked you that is because I didn't even ask you and you said --

A.   Well, I knew what you were thinking. You've got a dirty little mind, haven't you? Ah, shame on you! Yes, uh, it was a preoccupation. It also built up his trust in me more.

Q.   Violence and sex often go together, that's why I was going to ask.

A.   Sure they do. Sure they do. Uh, I kept wishing that he would be better sexually because, you know, I heard this story that he was quite a ladies' man. I don't know what them other women like, what they expect out of a guy, but he don't fill the bill, at all. He's very inadequate, but I might be inadequate, likewise, so my judgment is all my personal estimate of what I think. That's true of anything that you do in life. You have your own personal thought line.

137

(After this quote Joe's manly image of himself suffered greatly. The bailiff told me the inmates in the county jail gave him the nickname "Zero" after hearing her rating of his sexual prowess. They taunted him with that name until his transfer to the state penitentiary.)

Q. After that evening, then, until the time that the police apprehended you, what went through your mind? Were you concerned about being caught, did you think you might be caught?

A. Oh yeah, I thought I might be caught, but (unintelligible) enjoyable. Not being caught, but I was very apprehensive about the whole thing for a while. I was worried about, I watched first for them to find the bodies. They didn't find anything. This happened on a Saturday, that'd be Saturday, Sunday, Monday, Tuesday, Wednesday. Six days later they found the car and stuff, is when it hit the newspapers. I'm sure that the sheriff's department found the car way before then but they just didn't tell TV. They had this big search going for the bodies, this that and the other. I sat there and laughed about it.

Q. I remember that from the --

A. Yeah. I just said you stupid son-of-a-bitch, you ain't gonna ever find 'em. And then, Joe began to worry me, because you know, he was nervous and just -- I thought, well there's gonna be some trouble.

Q. Why didn't you kill then, Joe that is, because -- ?

A. Because I was afraid we were being watched by the police department or the FBI or somebody like this, so I felt like, you know, any movement I made right then would be watched. I even took the kids to the show and, uh, I don't remember what I took them to see, disgusting, wasn't good for kids to see, been all right for a couple to go, you know.

Q. Did you tell anyone what you had done besides your husband?

A.   No. I kept telling, it's just horrifying; it's a shocking thing to have happen in our area. I even, the day he was arrested, I went to his stepmother's and talked to her and tried to kind of pad the way because I knew that Joe was going to get picked up because of his previous trouble with these people, so I tried to pad the way so that they wouldn't think Joe was involved in it, by telling them that I was with Joe, that we went to the beach, that this and the other, that I had intentions of marrying him. Like shit I did. Uh, that, uh, that we were together all that evening and that Joe couldn't have possibly done it. I think they believed me halfway.

Q.   Did that story ever get back to your husband?

A.   Which one?

Q.   About intentions of marrying?

A.   No -- well, yeah, but he didn't think anything of it, didn't make him any difference. I think right now he would give his front seat in hell if he could get rid of me. Can't blame him. And I pretty well feel that way about him too. It's time to move on to someone else, to something else, because there's nothing there, oh I mean I love him, but there is no future, there is no, it'll be a re-enactment of what has already happened.

Q.   Do you think that you will ever have a fear of him telling someone?

A.   No, he's not that stupid. Because he would be an accessory to the crime. He knew about it before and after. He's no fool. That's just as....he's as guilty as I am if he opens his mouth.

I turned and scanned the audience. Leo had heard his name mentioned in the media and show up in enough newspaper accounts to know he was being watched. Shielding himself, again Leo's head went down and he raised his hand to his forehead to cover his face even further.

And that irony was not lost on the reporters. It was not Leo who was her undoing, it was her attorneys. Without the tape everything tying Linda to the case would be hearsay and inadmissible evidence. Joe could have turned on her and spilled his guts giving second-by-second testimony of her involvement in the murders and it would not have made any difference. The D.A. did not have any evidence that linked her to the crime. Nothing. Nada. Without the tape she would not even have been indicted by a grand jury. As I learned later, if Joe had not accidentally let her name slip out while taking officers to the grave site, they never would have known he had an accomplice.

Q.   Okay, and just to make sure, your name is pronounced Burnett?

A.   Burnett, not Barnett.

Q.   Burnett, Linda Burnett. Okay Linda.

The next sound was the "click" of the tape player being turned off.

The courtroom was silent. I immediately scanned the room for reactions. Some in the crowd were shaken and wiping away tears. Several jurors had watery eyes. Most of the audience sat there with blank looks on their faces as if a bomb had just gone off in front of them and they were shell-shocked. A few in the crowd whispered quietly. Every reporter was writing furiously for the next deadline. Leo sat there with a stoic expression. On the other side of the aisle members of the Phillips family had a look of deep pain and anger. Carver and Howell sat beside Linda at the defense table. Their faces did not reveal their thoughts or emotions. It was a calculated and valiant effort to give the impression the tape was not that big of a deal. I felt like I fit into the shell-shocked group. I did not feel like I was part of the history of a hypnotic confession allowed into evidence. I felt like a witness to a crime.

There were only two people in the courtroom who were still cool and nonchalant about the whole thing. They were sitting at the State's table, McGrath and Flatten. Now I knew why McGrath had been so cocky and sure of himself all along. Linda had in the most intricate detail laid out exactly what happened to the Phillips family.

And her attorneys had gift wrapped it and presented it to McGrath. Once he got the tape into evidence, McGrath knew there was no way he could lose the case. She had even told them where to look to find the corroborating evidence, even naming Fred Guzzardo, cluing in McGrath to subpoena him as a witness. And it was also evident why McGrath passionately hated Linda and wanted to personally be responsible for her being sentenced to death. The tape also gave McGrath an extra dose of cockiness. Not only did it seal the fate of Linda, it also gave him everything he needed to convict Joe as well even though McGrath said publicly convicting Joe would be much easier than Linda. There was also a possibility that after the tape was played Linda might agree to a plea bargain and testify against Joe if she could get a lighter sentence from the court. Because once the tape was played, death by lethal injection was the most likely scenario.

After the tape all the defense could do was try some attempts at damage control. The defense tried to prove all of the tape was made under hypnosis and that hypnosis is not a reliable tool for getting at the truth. They put Dr. G.W. Graham, a Beaumont Neurological Center clinical psychologist on the stand to testify that statements made under hypnosis are not necessarily the absolute truth. By the oddest of coincidences, I went to him about a year before for hypnosis to do a past life regression and now he was testifying that statements made under hypnosis are not necessarily true. *Not necessarily true?* I wondered if I should catch him in the hall and ask for a refund for my session.

Linda was put on the stand. She testified she did not know who the person was on the tape but she knew without a doubt it was not her voice, although everyone in the courtroom had just heard the tape, was now listening to her, and was satisfied that both voices came from her.

By then the State did not care that much about what the defense tried. The tape was played. The mystery was gone. Every word was now in the court record. The jury had heard every word on the tape. They had played their ace and knew the defense did not have a trump card. After the tape everyone in the court was certain they knew what happened to the Phillips, to Bishop, his wife Ester, their son Elmer, their daughter-in-law Martha, and their grandson Jason. And once they read about it in the paper or heard the story on TV or radio, everyone in Southeast Texas was confident the case was solved. The was only one question left, would the jury convict her?

I nervously bit the inside of my mouth and started putting phrases together in my head. My eyes were darting all over the audience for reactions. I was gathering all the facts, the emotions, the mood in the courtroom, and the explosive power of what I had just heard as I quickly slipped out of the courtroom to go to a live shot. It was always an exhilarating experience to break into regular programming for a live report, but this time it was tough picking out the right words to convey the experience of being an ear witness to murder. The two other stations also went live and the 3 of us rattled off details of the tape as quickly as possible. Down the hall radio reporters were grabbing secretaries' phones to get their live reports on. It was anticipation, theater, news, and drama converging into the fight to be first on the air. It was one of those adrenalin highs that I dreamed about when covering the usual daily mundane events we routinely packaged as news.

The adrenalin rush and high that comes with it only lasted until the next morning when I showed up at the courthouse. I had to take some kidding and outright ridicule, mostly from reporters, but also lawyers, and others at the courthouse. Walking down the hallway to court and in every break during the day, I heard catcalls such as,

"Roger. Killing is fun? Oh come on. Get real."

"Roger Daniel - Reporting for over the top news!"

"Hey Roger, when are you and your girlfriend Linda going to go out and have some fun?"

Fortunately the source of the ribbing and ridicule did not

come from my reporting. I did my live shot the afternoon before and then my story for the 6 o'clock news. Later, writing the copy for the evening news breaks, Bill Huston, our anchor and producer of the ten o'clock news, went over the events of the day and grabbed the most sensational lines for a news tease to promo our ten o'clock news. At least four times leading up to the 10 o'clock newscast that night in the middle of prime time programming, our viewers heard our newsbreak music followed by Bill on the news set blurting out the promo headline, ***"Linda May says killing is fun! Details at ten."***

CHAPTER TWELVE

Final Arguments

The playing of the tape the day before had drained much of the drama and doubt from the trial, but it still was not a done deal. A professor of mine in college put it very succinctly when he said, "Forget the facts, a jury can do whatever it wants." The next morning I was back in the courtroom as the State and defense made their final arguments. Under Texas law, the State goes first, then the defense is allowed one last attempt to persuade the jury of an innocent verdict, then the State has the last word before the jury leaves to deliberate. A small wooden podium was placed in front of the jury so both sides could put their notes on it and stand directly in front of the jury and look each one of them directly in the eyes as they made their final summations and admonitions to the jurors.

I was interested to see how Linda looked after the devastation of the tape. She sat there with her Bible and the case for her glasses in her hands. For final arguments she selected another new dress with a white silky scarf around her neck. It was one of the rare times she was not wearing one of her wigs, opting to go with her short, straight, stringy, brown hair, unlike the stylish hairstyle she had when first arrested. It was 9:25. For tactical reasons, and to have the last word, the State waived its right to go first and let the defense make the opening statements. By waiving its right, the State gives up a lot of time to make its case, but it puts the defense in the position of having to anticipate what the State will say, and then have no chance afterwards to refute what has been said. And it leaves the State in the very favorable position of having their arguments and their words ringing in the ears of the jurors when they leave the jury box to deliberate.

For the first time in the trial the remaining Phillips sons, Noel and George were together in the courtroom along with their family members and friends.

Erwing, who by this time was reinstated by the state bar association, got up to address the jury. "As you have clearly heard throughout this trial, the State has harassed witnesses. The State has used illegal tactics in getting evidence and people to trial."

Erwing tried to warn the jury about what the State would be doing when it had its turn to speak. I heard it in every trial I had ever covered. The defense has to do its best to defuse some of the inflammatory statements they know the state will use in its final arguments.

Erwing spoke in a conversational tone, as if appealing to the more deliberate and thoughtful side of the jurors. "The district attorney has tried the entire time to manipulate you into wanting revenge. They have done it with wild accusations. I expect them to shout and in a tirade try to enrage you to convict. The district attorney just wants to appeal to your emotion. The district attorney just wants to get your emotions agitated to the point of you acting irrationally. And the district attorney's office will distort the facts to try to get you to that emotional pitch."

For the final time the defense tried to put Joe, not Linda, on trial. "The personality of Joe Dugas looms over this trial." Once again Erwing insinuated that it was Joe, not Linda who put the Phillips family in their grave.

145

Erwing spoke for less than thirty minutes. Howell followed for about two minutes, mostly summarizing Helmut's legal points. Then Carver made the defense's final plea before the State took over. One of the intricate parts of covering a trial is to survey and gage the court. It sometimes helps you stay alert when a trial gets into the boring details. That morning as I looked around while Carver spoke, my eye caught Linda's great defense team at work. The defense table was less than ten feet from the jury box, at a 90 degree angle where every juror could plainly see every member of the defense team. Erwing was nodding off in his chair! I could not believe it. I was baffled. His eyes were closed and his head was slowly dropping. *Was this another curious defense tactic, or because he was really that unconcerned about the outcome of the trial? He couldn't stay awake at ten o'clock in the morning? Was his twenty minutes of defending Linda so uninteresting that it even put him to sleep?* I shook my head and scribbled the detail in my reporter's notebook.

While Erwing nodded off the gravity of the situation was weighing heavy on others. In the third row on the side of the defense table, Linda's sister sat in the audience, crying.

"'I heard a car pull up,'" Carver reminded the jury, referring to testimony that Charlie Neal, a friend of Joe - somehow through preplanning by Joe and Charlie - arrived at the death scene and was the actual killer who helped Joe carry out the murders.

"Linda is right. She never saw anything that happened. It was Joe and Charlie Neal who put the Phillips in that grave." Trying his best to weave an alternate conspiracy story, without Linda, Carver continued, "Joe and Charlie had to get Linda out there to the scene to make her a part of it. They tricked her so she would be an accessory and have to keep quiet."

In my mind Carver did a good job but after the tape I thought there was no way the case was salvageable. And at this point the best Carver could argue that she was only an accessory.

Flatten opened for the State, taking a low-key approach and

reiterating key evidence and testimony. When he finished McGrath took over. Erwing was right about one thing, McGrath began with all the emotion and fervor of a hell-fire and brimstone preacher. I knew McGrath wanted this conviction with a passion. He truly despised Linda. He made it clear off-camera he not only hated her, he hated her on behalf of every person in Southeast Texas who wanted the State to put a needle in her arm. He would have gladly offered his services to personally be the one to do it.

It was noon when McGrath began. I had never seen him make closing arguments and was not sure what to expect. He did not even warm up. He grabbed the podium with both hands. Like an evangelical preacher in a tent revival he unleashed the fires of hell on the jury. He started about two decibels above his normal speaking voice and got louder from there. His voice quivered as he shouted, ranted, and again and again, thrust his forefinger with force towards Linda as he called her name. With his teeth clenched and jaw muscles bulging McGrath attacked the facts of the case in a take-no-prisoners approach. He began a tirade that never let up for more than thirty minutes. He hollered, he yelled, he beat his fists on the podium and even pounded his fists on the defense table with a defiant, in-your-face confrontation of Linda and her lawyers. I was surprised the defense did not object to some of his theatrics. They were way over the top and clearly intended to inflame the jurors with the same hatred for Linda that McGrath had. He was true to his promise to fire every shot in his gun to get a conviction. Slightly lowering his voice and changing his cadence, he went over the gruesome details of the Phillips' bodies when they were recovered, their position in the grave, where they were shot, and how 3-year-old Jason was shot with his arms tightly wrapped around his father's neck. It was graphic, it was disgusting, and it was a masterful touch. There were people all over the audience crying.

McGrath was in full attack mode. "When the state ruled on capital murder they had her in mind. I think it would have been fitting for her and Joe Dugas to exhume those five bodies, except I wouldn't want their filthy hands to touch the bodies. Even as bad as Joe Dugas is, in my opinion he's a saint compared to this woman." Looking straight at Linda with a scowl on his face, McGrath looked like he was going to jump on her like a trained attack dog. You could see the veins in his neck bulging out. "She thrives on violence. She says sex and violence go together."

His tactics worked. If he had been preaching in church there would be shouts of "amen, brother" coming from all over the audience. One of the women in the jury box was crying and wiping away the tears as McGrath continued with his tirade.

Turning from the podium and the jury, McGrath walked over and leaned on the defense's table with his face turning and even deeper red and snarled, "Don't let her go back down to Nederland and associate with decent people." In the audience Linda's sister let out an audible moan. "Don't ever let her ever again influence her three daughters," McGrath yelled at the jury. With that admonition every one in the courtroom heard Linda's sister's tears burst into gut-wrenching sobs.

It was a great sales job that even McGrath was buying. It was as if the crying from Linda's relatives only further fueled his determination for a conviction. He never wavered. He never let up. With tears in his eyes McGrath walked from the podium to all the pieces of evidence admitted into the trial and picked up one of the pictures from inside the Phillips's house. In the picture was a rocking horse that was in the Phillips's home the night they disappeared. It was a rocking horse Bishop and Ester kept for 3-year-old Jason's visits from Oklahoma.

McGrath held the picture in his left hand and angrily thrust it towards the jury and yelled, "See that rocking horse? Little Jason will never ride it again." Quickly swinging his body and right arm to the right and piercing the air emphatically as he again jabbed his index finger directly at Linda, McGrath screamed, "*Because she killed him!*"

With those words ringing through the courtroom McGrath

turned and sat down. My eyes darted over the audience. There were tears and audible crying all through the audience. One of the women in the jury box was crying. Linda was crying so hard she was on the verge of totally breaking down. The muffled sobs and sniffling through tears continued as Judge Gist read his instructions to the jury. At 12:35 the jurors were escorted back to the jury room to begin deliberations. After the jury left Linda lost it completely and two deputies led her out of the courtroom sobbing.

The radio reporters immediately ran for the door to grab a phone to call in a report. I went outside to tell the live crew where we were so they could relay the information back to the station. Then along with the two other TV reporters and newspaper writers, I went into a back room near the judge's office. It was large enough to accommodate more than a dozen reporters and photographers assembled for the day. It was also out of earshot of the jury deliberation room so we did not have to worry about disturbing the jury's deliberations.

I covered all types of stories, including the gruesome, the macabre, the disgusting, and the disturbing, along with the dull and boring everyday city council meetings. It does not take long before you develop a bit of callousness in order to keep your sanity. The real pros at it however, are the police. I remember one morning about 11 o'clock my photographer and I went to a murder scene to get a statement and video of the body being removed from the apartment where the crime was committed. Shortly before noon an investigator came out to give us a statement. He said that in all of his many years of experience he had never seen such a brutal murder and gruesome crime scene. He said it was gory, nasty, ugly, and heinous. Then he left us to go pick up lunch. Five minutes later he came back with a bag of burgers and took them inside to this gory, nasty, ugly, and heinous one-bedroom crime scene, to eat lunch with the other two investigators, and the brutally murdered body of the deceased.

As a group the reporters in the waiting room probably had at least a half century of experience, with a lot of it covering trials. It was past the noon newscasts for both TV and radio so we had time on our hands. And as reporters do with time on their hands, began speculating.

"I bet they'll have a verdict before five this afternoon."

"Quicker than that."

"I don't know, there's a lot of evidence."

"I bet it will take longer than that."

"How much you willing to bet?"

"Oh, I could go as high as a dollar."

"Let's get up a pool."

"Yeah!" three voices chimed in.

"Okay, a dollar for the time they come back out. A dollar. Fair enough?"

A dollar was a lot of money for all of us. Reporters in the smaller radio and TV markets work for the experience more than the money. I was one of the most senior reporters in the group and I was not even cracking the $20,000 mark. So before anyone suggested a bigger ante, everyone agreed, threw in a dollar and wrote down the time they were betting we would have a verdict. I was the most optimistic of the group and bet we would have a verdict in two hours.

The pool started with eleven dollars in the pot. We bet on the time we thought it would take the jury to reach a verdict. You bet on a time and once your time was past, you were out of the running. One of the newspaper reporters, who had to be there all night if necessary, became the official scorekeeper and money holder. The pot grew larger during the following hours as clerks, secretaries, and lawyers wandering through got in on the wagering. Funny thing, the only wager was on the time when the jury would reach a verdict. Nobody was betting on an innocent verdict.

Time dragged on and after we all recapped our favorite parts of the trial, stories began to surface about other cases and trials. My contribution was a story related to me by Bo Horka, the district

150

attorney in Hardin County, just north of Jefferson County in Southeast Texas.

As Horka related the story, he made his final arguments in a murder trial and the jury went into the deliberation room. The Hardin County courthouse was built for a rural county, i.e., built as cheaply as possible. It was small and the walls were thin. After about thirty minutes Horka and the lawyers heard laughing inside the deliberation room. They heard loud talking and the jurors apparently having a good old time.

The sounds of a good time continued for a couple of hours until the foreman sent word they had reached a verdict. They came back in and issued a guilty verdict and sentenced the defendant to death. Horka was delighted with the verdict but still puzzled by what he heard. After the verdict was read and the jury dismissed he approached the foreman of the jury.

"I couldn't help but wonder during the deliberation why you all were laughing in the jury room," Horka asked. "This was murder. A man's life was at stake. Why were you laughing in there?"

The foreman answered, "After going through instructions required by law, we had been in there about ten minutes, and then it only took us about ten more to agree he was guilty. We didn't want the verdict overturned on a technicality by some lawyer saying we didn't give credible deliberation to the man's fate. So we voted him guilty and discovered we'd been in there less than thirty minutes total. We decided to stay back in the jury room a couple of hours to make it appear we had given the evidence the utmost of our deepest concern and had with stern deliberation reached a guilty verdict. So," the foreman told an astonished Horka, "we just sat back there and told jokes and visited for about an hour and a half."

This jury was not laughing. They were separated from us by distance and soundproof walls. They were not making any sounds we could hear. We had no indications that deliberations were going smoothly, acrimoniously, quickly, or slowly. By 3 p.m. it was decision time for me and the newsroom. Rather than risk getting caught back at the station when a verdict came in, we decided I would stay at the courthouse and my six o'clock report would be a live shot with me and the anchor talking to one another. In effect, the anchor would interview me and I would recount the events of the trial up to that point, speculate about when we could expect a verdict, and then assure our viewers that I would be right there to give them an instantaneous report as soon as we knew a verdict. We decided that would be our game plan for the six o'clock, then I would stay at the courthouse for either a verdict or adjournment, then go back to the newsroom and put together a story for the ten o'clock news. Once we decided that, I slipped away down the hall to the District Clerk's office and made a quick call home to let my wife know she should eat supper without me.

The jury was not as astute, or calloused as the reporters. They went past all the bets of everyone in the pool. They went past the six o'clock news and into the evening. I was the first one out with my two hour bet. The winner of the pool was a reporter from a Lake Charles, Louisiana, station who guessed there would be a verdict by early evening. No one bet the jury would go past eight o'clock that night. The jury went past six, then seven, and then they asked to break for the night and the judge obliged. He ordered them sequestered and to be back at nine o'clock in the morning to resume their deliberations.

The jurors may not have tried to prolong the deliberations to give the impression of being fair like Horka's jury, but all was not as it appeared on the surface. Before the deliberations began, the jury had already spent many hours together in the jury room talking and getting to know one another, because until the deliberation phase, they are not allowed to talk about the trial. After the trial multiple sources acknowledged to me that a romance broke out on the jury and the woman involved wanted to extend the jury's time together as long as possible. According to my sources, she was not being difficult and arguing with the rest of the jury, she was just being obstinate so she could spend more time with the guy she had a crush on. When I heard that I felt cheated and wanted my dollar back.

More disturbing, I was told a few months after the trial about another incident that could have destroyed everything. As I was told by a bailiff actually at the scene and a witness to the event, after the judge ordered the jury sequestered, a couple of jurors snuck out of the motel where they were staying. They did not go far, just out in the parking lot where they were smoking some pot one of them had in his car. Rather than risk the tens of thousands of dollars already spent on the trial and cause a really unpleasant situation for the jurors, the judge, the D.A.'s office, and the entire county legal system, plus put a real black mark on all past and future juries in Jefferson County, the two were quickly and quietly escorted back to their room. Their marijuana stash was seized, destroyed, and quickly forgotten. The guilty jurors were threatened with jail time of their own if they tried that trick again.

Fortunately it only took one night of being sequestered to help bring the jury to a verdict. Back in court the next morning events moved quickly. Before ten o'clock the jury sent a message by the bailiff that they had reached a verdict. All the attorneys were notified to get to the courtroom. We already had our camera and live truck set up, so it was just a matter of a radio call to put every necessary technician on standby. Ted had his coat and tie on, ready to walk on to the news set and pitch the newscast to me live at the scene.

With my pen and reporters' notebook in hand and my nerves still juiced from the morning's coffee and the anticipation of a verdict, I joined all the reporters, lawyers, secretaries, and the public as we surged like a herd of cattle and squeezed through the door anxiously going back into the courtroom to wait for the jury.

Even though for the past several days a metal detector and 3 more deputies had become a new fixture in the trial, Judge Gist announced to the courtroom that he would not tolerate any outbursts of any kind, pro or con, at the announcement of the verdict. Anyone doing so would be arrested and held in contempt of court. The extra armed deputies, who made their first appearance in the courtroom around the judge, the jury, the audience and inside and outside of all the doors, clearly emphasized how serious he was about maintaining order in his courtroom. Judge Gist was keyed into the emotional pitch and never took anything for granted. In addition to two armed officers in the court whenever it was in session, no matter how mundane the case or how timid the temperament of the defendant, I knew Judge Gist also kept a loaded .38 revolver in his desk drawer within easy reach whenever his court was in session. And for backup, on or off the bench, he always had a six shot derringer in his right boot.

After his warning to the spectators, Judge Gist turned to the jury and asked if they had reached a decision. The foreman stood, turned to the judge and answered "yes." Judge Gist instructed the foreman to hand the verdict to the court clerk, Judy Gant, and asked her to read the jury's decision.

Ten weeks of testimony and motions, and it was down to one sentence in an envelope handed down by the eight men and four women on the jury. The bailiff took the envelope and handed it to Gant. The court was so quiet that even in the large courtroom you could hear the crinkle of the paper as it changed hands from the foreman to Gant.

Gant knew her judge very well and that he did not like courtroom theatrics from the audience or his staff. She took the paper and read it slowly, clearly and succinctly to make sure she got every word right. She was just a few inches over five feet tall and probably weighed less than a hundred pounds. In a voice bigger than its source Gant bellowed out, "We the jury... find the defendant... Linda May Burnett... At that point everyone in the courtroom held their collective breath. After ten weeks of courtroom testimony and drama, no one wanted to make any sound that would keep them from hearing the decision. Without any change in the emotion or pitch of her voice, Gant finished, "Guilty as charged."

There were a few audible sighs and moans as well as some

Burnett family members crying, and some hushed sounds of "YES" as the remaining members of the Phillips family listened to the verdict across the aisle from Linda's family.

In the reporters' section notepads were furiously flipped and partial sentences hastily scrawled down. I was ready to step outside as soon as Judge Gist dismissed the court. A couple of the radio reporters headed for the door even though court was still in session. I was not that concerned about getting scooped because I knew my crew in the hall would see the look on the reporters' faces as they raced out of the courtroom and know that the verdict was in. Every television reporter had instructions to get on the air as quickly as possible. Before I stepped into the hall my crew had our live equipment set up, warmed up, calibrated, and pictures microwaved back to the station. While the jury deliberated I had written down my story so I would be prepared to run out and confidently begin a report. The slowest part of the equation was for our anchor Ted to get his coat on, tighten his tie, put his mike on, and the director to flip a switch breaking into programming. It was probably the only live report in Southeast Texas history that no one called to complain about their favorite program being interrupted.

As soon as I knew the judge was not going to say anything else more dramatic than the verdict, I made my way outside as well, walking and putting my earpiece in as I headed towards the door. As soon as I was connected to audio, I heard our newsbreak theme music playing in my earpiece, followed by the voice of Ted saying, "Good morning. The jury has just returned a verdict in the trial of Linda May Burnett. Our reporter, Roger Daniel is at the courthouse where we now take you live. Roger, what was the jury's decision?"

This was why I wanted to be a television news reporter. There was commotion all around me but my focus was directly into the lens below the blinding bright light on our camera. Around me was a swirl of lawyers, conflicting camera lights, flash cameras, microphone cords, camera cables duct taped down to the tile floor, and curious court watchers inside a whirlpool of the emotionally charged moment. Radio reporters added to the sounds of dozens of different conversations being broadcast simultaneously. It was chaos as quickly all 3 TV stations were going live and as we barked out details of the verdict. With marble walls, tile flooring and plaster ceiling in the hallway, there was nothing to absorb the sound. The sound of excited conversations and news reports bounced off the walls and back into the hallway creating a cacophony of clashing noise. In the center of it all I looked directly into the camera lens and into the eyes of every person in our viewing audience watching and waiting for details. There was bedlam all around me but my feet were solidly planted in the living room of every viewer. My heart beat rapidly as my veins pumped all the adrenalin my body could produce. I knew I had the undivided attention of every viewer and their heart rates were also increasing as they had put aside whatever they were doing in anxious anticipation of what I was about to say.

Years earlier I was a radio news reporter at a news conference for my station and saw the impact of the television camera. No matter what the occasion or who is involved, a TV camera and its bright light is a commanding presence not given to newspaper reporters with a pen and pencil, or a radio reporter holding a cassette and a little microphone. Flip on the camera light and the person being interviewed immediately takes on a whole new demeanor, their posture changes, the look on their faces suddenly gets more serious and their words become much more calibrated. I saw that and at that moment I knew I wanted to be a TV reporter. Fortunately for me as a TV reporter, for those reasons and others, lawyers are attracted to bright lights and the red light on cameras. They know that when the red light comes on, it is showtime.

In my right hand I had my microphone and in my left hand I had a firm grip on McGrath's arm, holding on to make sure no other reporter or station took him away from me. He was the talking head, the quote machine every reporter wanted. I had him first and was not going to let anyone butt in on my courthouse coup.

"Ted, after more than six hours of deliberation last night and this morning the jury found thirty one year old Linda May Burnett guilty of the murder of three-year-old Jason Phillips, one of the five Phillips family members murdered last summer in Winnie........

CHAPTER THIRTEEN

Sentencing

"So what happens now?" Bill MacAtee was our sports anchor. It was his first job in TV and he was vaguely following the trial.

"Well, there are two parts to a capital murder trial in Texas," I began. "First the jury makes a decision on guilty or innocent. If it's innocent then the trial is over. In a trial of just one murder the State has no appeal if it loses. But in this case there were five murders."

"But it's only one crime."

"Not in this case. One crime, but five murders. The beauty of this case for the State is that they have five cases to use against her and Dugas. By separating Linda and Joe's cases, the State has the possibility of going to court ten times to get two convictions."

"The judge can't step in and say one way or the other if there can be other trials?"

"No. In Texas all a judge does is preside over the hearings, maintain order in the courtroom, and rule on objections of the lawyers. For instance, if one side says something that's speculation or not supported by evidence, and the other side doesn't object, then it goes into the record. If either one side objects to something said, then the judge can sustain the objection and disallow the statement, or overrule it and let the statement into evidence. The only other thing a Texas criminal judge can do is prod the lawyers to move along if it appears they're trying to stall or draw out the proceedings. In federal court a judge can interject at any time and ask questions himself."

"What about the sentence. Does the judge do that? "

"Not in Texas. If the jury decides the defendant is guilty then the jury also decides the sentence. In a capital murder case in Texas the jury has two choices; life in prison or death by lethal injection."

At that point I could see Bill's eyes beginning to glaze over so I kept on gathering my pens and pads to go to the courthouse, and let Bill get back to his world of sports where he was more comfortable.

About fifteen minutes later I was downtown and in the courtroom along with the regular reporters and a packed courtroom. Although we had our verdict, there was one other possibility bigger than Joe Dugas looming over the trial. In Texas there is one other option that the district attorney and the residents of the county hate. Although I have never seen it happen and it is unlikely, it was a possibility and a dread of everyone in the county. It was possible the jury could deadlock on the punishment. When that happens the judge is forced to declare a mistrial. That means even though they found her guilty, the entire trial is thrown out and the process starts all over again. Another jury is selected and the whole trial put on as if the first trial never happened. It is a very lengthy and expensive alternative that is demoralizing for the State's lawyers and outrages county tax payers. The pocketbook aspect of a trial is an unspoken fact of our justice system. I heard jurors say many times, thinking about the cost to the county helped persuade a reluctant juror to capitulate so they could reach a verdict to avoid wasting their time, and the taxpayers' money.

Once a person is found guilty the State puts on witnesses to prove the defendant has a record of violent behavior, and if given the opportunity, will continue to commit more acts of violence. I had seen it many times and knew what to expect. The State calls to the stand people who know from first hand experience what a terrible person the defendant was, is, and will be.

To counter that the defense brings out all the friends, family, preachers, school teachers, respected members of the community, etc., it can round up who will testify about the good things the defendant has done. This is an attempt to show the defendant has some redeeming qualities and should have their life spared. Also the defense puts on the stand their expert psychologist who testifies there is no way you can accurately predict future human behavior based on what has transpired in the past, no matter how heinous the crime. Then very predictably, the State counters with their expert psychologist who unequivocally states that past behavior is the only indicator of future behavior. One very well known psychologist in Southeast Texas testified for the State so many times that defense attorneys nicknamed him "Dr. Death."

If the jury agrees with the State then they must sentence the defendant to death. If the jury thinks this was just one instance where the defendant committed a violent crime and probably will never do so again then the sentence is life in prison. Sometimes juries decide the murder was a one-time event when the person was pushed over the edge by events beyond their control, such as a spouse catching their mate in bed with someone and in a fit of rage, killing them. In a situation like that the jury may decide the defendant did not have a predisposition to commit murder again and sentence them to life in prison.

All through the trial the defense warned the jury not to let their emotions sway them. But when it came down to life or death the defense was not above playing directly to the emotions either. For one of their final pleas, the defense brought Linda's daughter Nora Jane into the courtroom and put her on the witness stand. Again, searching for that one juror who could be emotionally swayed, Carver began with questioning Nora Jane about her age, to make sure the jury knew it was an eleven year old child on the stand, and as an added emotional heart-tug, the day before her twelfth birthday. *Nice touch Carver, as I thought about the implied nuance, "and now members of the jury, what are you going to give this child for her birthday? Her mother? Or will it be, 'Happy Birthday Janie. We're killing your mother."* Not the least bit subtle, but when a life and death debate is underway, nothing is sacred.

"Janie, do you know what is the purpose of the jury next to you on your left?" Carver continued.

"To see whether or not my mother gets the death penalty," she answered in her youthful innocence.

It was a strange sight and an uncomfortable one for everyone involved. About six feet away from her were twelve jurors looking at a child who knew they could kill her mother. A couple of the jurors squirmed in discomfort. In Carver's favor, he did not have to sway all twelve. All he had to do was get one juror to refuse a death sentence. He was making his appeal hoping to reach that one juror. A mistrial is a win for the defense.

The State had some family members to put on the stand as well. One was Linda's former husband Hubert Miller and the father of two of her daughters. An old looking man, with struggling movements, Miller limped to the witness stand as if it was taking all the energy he could muster. Linda watched with tears rolling down her face as he slowly braced himself against the railing and, as if in agony, lowered himself into the witness chair.

Miller was married 3 times before he married Linda. He had married again since their divorce. And apparently, judging from his testimony, I would say there divorce was definitely not an amicable one. But of the four divorces, this one had really left an indelible scar on him, physically and mentally.

"After your divorce," Flatten asked, "did Linda ever come into your house again?"

"Yes."

"Could you tell the jury what happened that day she came to your house?"

"She just walked into my living room," Miller answered as if a full sentence completely winded him.

"Did she say anything, did she do anything?"

"I asked, 'what are you doing here?'"

"And what did she say?"

"She didn't say anything. She just pulled out a pistol and shot me in the shoulder."

"She just shot you without saying anything?"

"Just shot me. I still have the slug in my shoulder."

"Was anybody with her?"

"Her husband, Leo. He was waiting for her out in the car."

"You and Linda had some problems before, didn't you? At one point didn't you shoot at Linda when she was seven months pregnant with your child and didn't you hit her knocking some of her teeth out?"

"No, I never did those things."

"Well then how do you explain the doctor's report of her being treated for a gunshot wound?"

"She shot herself."

It was a pretty incredulous statement that brought some muffled giggles from the reporters' section, but debating the logic behind it would not help make Flatten's point of showing the violent tendencies of Linda, so he switched directions with his questions. Also not arguing the very unlikely scenario helped Flatten. If Linda is crazy enough to shoot herself, this woman really is a threat to society.

"After Linda walked into your living room and shot you, what did she do next?"

"She took me to the hospital."

"Hubert, after you and Linda divorced, did you ever change her as the beneficiary on your insurance policy?"

"No."

"And you've remarried since your divorce. Why haven't you changed her as your beneficiary?"

"Because I still love her to this day."

That one really brought out giggles and groans all over the court room. And it helped Flatten show that Linda was some sort of redneck psychopath who shoots 'em but by God, she still loves 'em.

"No further questions. We pass the witness."

At one that afternoon Judge Gist read the second set of charges to the jury. He told the jury they had to decide if the crime was committed deliberately and if the jurors believed the defendant would continue to be a menace to society. After that the final arguments began for sentencing.

Walking up to the small podium before the jury, Erwing began the defense's final plea.

"Ladies and gentlemen," Erwing opened, "the State has brought no evidence to this courtroom to show that Linda will continue to act violently." He continued twenty-four minutes longer presenting the legal reasons why she should not be given the death penalty and imploring the jury to spare her death by lethal injection. He even described the physical process of what happens when a human is given a lethal injection. He was trying to reach that one juror who would be so nauseated by the thought of taking a human life that the juror would steadfastly defy the others and vote for a life sentence instead. Erwing painted a very vivid and disgusting verbal picture of the needle going into the arm, and then the body's reaction as the poison spread to the muscles and internal organs, causing all the body systems to collapse with each step of the body collapsing dramatically described in deliberate detail.

I do not know if Erwing caught the irony, but his argument rang a little hollow when I remembered listening to the tape of Linda under hypnosis. She described it very clearly and never objected when Joe stuck a needle into four adults and injected them with roach poison. But as I sat there and thought of the description from a juror's point of view, I knew it was a very compelling argument, it was more than I wanted to know about death by lethal injection. But it certainly had to be more humane than the former Texas method, 'ol Sparky, the electric chair that would literally fry people with electricity.

Erwing did his part to try to make the jury members sick to their stomachs with gory details of the dying process, and then Carver took over and appealed to their logical minds. Once again he tried to get the jury to focus somewhere besides Linda. With one of the most obvious statements repeated over and over during the trial, Carver began his final plea for mercy.

"The shadow of Joe Dugas looms over this case and court," Carver reminded the jurors one more time. He pressed on making one last effort to raise doubt in the jurors about Linda's participation in the crime, insinuating once more that it was Joe and Charlie Neal who had the brawn and guts it would take to kill five people. He contrasted that by painting a picture of Linda as just a frail, innocent bystander sucked into the violent whirlpool swirling around her. He tried to get the jury to think it was Joe who was the evil one, not Linda. Carver made her to be a victim of circumstance, a victim of Joe Dugas' diabolical schemes against other people. Once again he mentioned Linda's testimony about a second set of headlights she saw on Highway 365. He was hoping those headlights would illuminate at least one juror who would not vote for the death sentence.

Carver concluded, and Flatten made the first remarks for the State describing a much different picture of Linda May for the jury. Using facts and much more animated than in the first phase of the trial, at times almost shouting, Flatten aimed his remarks to the emotions and inherent decency of the jurors.

"Linda May was the brains behind the murders. Joe and Charlie were buffoons. They were the brawn behind her brains. She wanted the bond sealed with blood. She wanted Joe to kill the baby so they would be in it fifty-fifty. It was Linda who had the clarity of mind to meticulously remove all the dirt from the shovels," Flatten told the jury, although that was an insinuation of the State and never proven. "She was the one to dispose of anything that could connect them to the crime and to cook up the alibis to use in case Joe became a suspect. She thought up the alibis. She's smart. She knew that with Joe's history of run-ins with the Phillips family he'd be the number one suspect immediately. She knew they'd be knocking on his door the next day. And she knew that no matter how suspect he was in the case, with no evidence and no bodies there would be no case."

Flatten glared at Linda, "Money was the motive," he continued with absolute disgust in his voice. "Greed. She was planning on getting the insurance money and social security benefits after Joe helped her kill her ex-husband Hubert Miller. They've tried everything to make you feel sympathetic to Linda. They even put her daughter on the stand to draw the milk of human kindness from you. Don't buy it. I think her children are already gone. It ain't my fault," Flatten broke into the vernacular to appeal to the jurors. "And it ain't your fault." He paused. He looked at Linda. He lowered his voice, "It's her fault," and slowly turned and sat down at the State's table.

McGrath gathered his papers for the State's final remarks. After his explosive closing arguments in the guilt phase of the trial, I was set for another high-decibel performance. Faster than he normally moves, McGrath rose from his seat like a thoroughbred out of the starting gate to make the last emotional pitch to the jury. McGrath's hatred for Linda had not abated during the course of the trial. He did not just hate her for what she had done; he hated her for what she was making him do. He had a cleanliness fetish. People who had witnessed it told me he would not even touch himself when he went to the bathroom. He got around that problem by using toilet paper to cover his hands so he could avoid contact with himself.

During the course of the trial McGrath was repulsed every time he had to touch the bags containing the ropes and tape the pathologist removed from the badly decomposed bodies. I knew about his phobia and smiled whenever he submitted anything into evidence. He did so by very gingerly touching the plastic bags using the smallest portion of his finger tips to hold only the smallest fraction of the corner of the bags. After he introduced them as evidence he ran out at the first break and went into the men's room to feverishly wash his hands. He detested anything unclean and decaying bodies buried in dirt turned his stomach. He despised the thought of it, was repulsed by pictures presented to the jury, and he had no love for anyone who had anything to do with it. This was not courtroom dramatics. He genuinely hated Linda for making him handle anything from the crime scene.

McGrath made no apologies for the trial. "I fought the change of venue because I wanted her tried here in Jefferson County where she deserves to be tried."

Linda had no love for McGrath either and as he talked she silently wiped away tears. Several others in the audience wept as McGrath laid out the gruesome details of the death and burial of the Phillips family. I glanced frequently and watched the remaining Phillips brothers; George and Noel Jr. stoically listen as McGrath put his entire emotional arsenal into the final argument.

With tears in his eyes McGrath looked at the jury, "I think it would have been fitting for her and Joe Dugas to exhume those five bodies, except I wouldn't want their filthy hands to touch those bodies. Even as bad as Joe Dugas is, in my opinion, he's just a sniveling coward compared to this woman," he said pointing at Linda.

With scorn in his voice he turned to the defense table. "I think you know why they brought those children up here. This is not a fit mother. This is a woman who will kill anyone who gets in her way, including a man who still loves her. What for? For lousy social security."

Suddenly McGrath turned away from the jury. It was an odd moment in the trial and incongruent with his closing arguments. I do not know why he did it; maybe it was just to show the jury that this was only the beginning of a house cleaning on crime in Jefferson County. Whatever his reason he suddenly spun around towards the spectators, and with his head bobbing around as if he was trying to find someone in particular, with a fierce fire burning in his eyes, McGrath shouted out to Linda's husband in the packed and stunned courtroom, "I'm not excluding you from this either, Leo!"

Still scowling and seething with rage he turned back to the jurors. "She thrives on violence," he scowled as he looked back at the jurors. "She says sex and violence go together."

With undisguised viciousness and hatred in his voice and words McGrath lashed into Linda. While she sat there crying, McGrath again pushed to the limit a reprimand by the judge for courtroom dramatics. With vengeance he left the podium and leaned on the defense table and shouted at her face, "When the State ruled death for capital murder, they had her in mind!"

Standing up straight and turning to face the jury again McGrath punched the air with his index finger pointing directly at Linda and shouted in a dramatic crescendo, "Don't ever let this evil woman have the chance of influencing her three daughters again."

It was over. Linda was crying silently into a Kleenex. Both sides had used all their allotted time. Now it was Judge Gist's time. He instructed the jurors that if they felt Linda would continue to commit crimes then the decision would be death by lethal injection. If they believed she would not commit further crimes then the decision would be life in prison. In Texas to get a death sentence all twelve jurors must vote yes on both the question of the defendant committing the crime deliberately and the defendant continuing to be a menace to society. Judge Gist gave final instructions and the jurors quietly and stoically filed out of the jury box.

If the jury voted for the death sentence it meant more appearances in court for Linda. Under Texas law, a death sentence is automatically appealed through the appellate court system. Which meant there could be several more mornings of Linda and me greeting one another across the courtroom. A life sentence meant Linda would have to serve at least twenty years before being eligible for parole. I knew that no matter what happened next, this was too big of a story to ignore, so I would be following the appeals process to Austin. That would include a road trip for me, staying in a hotel, enjoying life on the station's tab. There are not many perks that come with reporting so a road trip was a big deal.

The jury had been out for a few hours and there was a group of us reporters in the back room where we shot the bull, wrote multiple stories to cover every scenario, but mostly just sat around waiting for a verdict. All was going well until there were loud voices in the hallway, telling everyone to get back into the courtroom. A chill went through my body. It was a few minutes past five, just about the worst possible time for a decision. It meant we would have to go live, which would throw the entire 6 o'clock newscast out of sync, and require some quick rewriting of my story I had prepared. We quickly filed back into the courtroom to hear that the jury sent a note to the judge asking him to define the probability of, and when she could possibly get out on parole with a life sentence. The judge sent them a note back explaining that they could not factor those details into their decision. They had to make up their minds strictly on the basis of whether or not they thought she would continue to be a menace to society. As they did in the first phase of the trial the jury deliberated past the six o'clock news and into the evening. This time there was no betting. No one was willing to wager even a dollar as to how long it would take the jury to decide. Once again, as he had before, judge Gist adjourned them for the night and set the deliberations to resume the next morning.

Relieved that it was just a note and the jury had not reached a decision and forced my adrenalin into overdrive to get a story on the air, I grabbed my notepad and got to the hallway as quickly as possible. It was past five, too late to get back and put together a story for the 6 o'clock. We would have to stay put and do another live shot from the courthouse. I did the live shot wrapping up the day's events, and without saying it, I was just as disappointed as our viewers when I told them we had at least another day to wait before the jury made the final decision in the case. I went back to the station and put together a story for the ten o'clock news, then headed home for what had become reoccurring theme throughout the trial, a late supper. I was tired but glad that everything happened in a sequence that allowed me to put together a story and get it on the air without rushing. And although I was a little dejected that we did not get the news we had been waiting on for ten months, I was also a little happy that the drama was being drawn out for at least one more day. Once the trial was over, I knew it was back to city council meetings and chasing fire trucks to burning houses. And back to the boring, predictable, fill-in-the-blank stories I had written variations of, thousands of times.

Fortunately the next morning court did not convene until ten, so I did not have to revise my work schedule to accommodate the trial. I checked in at the station where we strategized for every possible scenario, and I was back at the courthouse by 9:30. It was my feeling, and that of several other reporters, that there would be a decision before the day was done. The morning began as it had so many times before, when Linda entered the courtroom with her defense team. As she had throughout the trial she glanced over to her right and silently said a "good morning" to me. This time there was no smile that went along with it. This was not a "good morning" and there was not much hope visible in her face or the faces of her attorneys.

With the same pattern as before the jury came back and after less than an hour of deliberation and before eleven o'clock voices started ringing up and down the hallway that the jury called for the bailiff to tell the judge they were ready to issue their verdict. I ran for the outside hall to tell my crew to radio the station that we were just moments away from a decision.

It took a few minutes to get more than 200 people through security so since reporters went in first; I had a chance to start working on some notes to use for a live shot. Again Judge Gist began with a warning to the courtroom about outbursts of emotion over the jury's decision. Again extra armed deputies with extra ammunition around their waists were stationed all over the courtroom. This was it. The final climatic moment in the trial.

I quickly scanned the courtroom for details I could use in my live shot that would help paint the scene for our viewers and depict the atmosphere when the verdict was announced. McGrath and Flatten looked relaxed and confident. At the defense table the mood was somber and stone faces. For the defense at this point even a life sentence was a victory.

The courtroom became quiet once again as the foreman passed the decision to the clerk to read to the court.

Although no one was speaking as we waited the decision, you could hear the sounds of a few in the audience starting to moan in anticipation of what was coming.

Gant, the court clerk, had long brown hair that extended to her waist. She rose, and when she reached for the foreman's note half of her hair fell over her shoulder. She took the note, tossed her head to her left putting her hair back into place. Facing the audience, in a firm and steady voice she read, "We the jury sentence the defendant Linda May Burnett to death by lethal injection," When the word 'death' came out of her mouth Gant's words quickly faded into the rising hum of murmurs, stifled cheers, and sobbing of Linda's supporters. Once again Linda burst into tears, crying uncontrollably. Carver had his arm around her shoulder trying to console her. At their table, McGrath and Flatten were trying desperately to look professional, but not giddy over the sentence.

I quickly scanned the scene once more looking for audience reactions I could use to put into my live shot. My mind was so caught up in hyper-drive thinking about the reaction in the courtroom that I hardly had time to think about how I felt. It was no surprise as I thought it was the only decision the jury could have made given the evidence. And as a reporter I was enjoying the moment because it was the most dramatic decision the jury could have reached. Linda was about to become the only woman on death row in Texas and possibly only the second woman to ever to die at the hands of the state. But I had to set those thoughts aside and get back to the business of going live as fast as possible.

There were a few more legal procedures the judge had to take care of before adjourning the court, but at that point my mind was racing with what I had to do and what I was going to say on air. It was the same routine as before for the reporters, rushing out into the hall and waiting for the cue from the station to start talking. Luck was with me that morning. Our equipment was all warmed up and on standby and Ted already had his coat and tie on back at the station, so we were the first to get a live shot from outside the courtroom. One of the members of our production department was assigned to the story. He handed me the microphone and started connecting the wire to the earpiece I was quickly forcing into my ear canal. As I got it in and securely looped the support bracket over my ear, I could hear Ted telling the audience the jury had reached a decision and he was taking them live to the courthouse where I was standing by. On cue I quickly set the scene in the hallway for our viewers and then, improvising as I went along about what had happened in the court and the reaction of the spectators, I waded through the throng of people making my way to Carver, Linda's lead attorney, who was talking to a radio reporter. On any other story it would have been rude for me to break into another reporter's interview but this day was different and any hurt feelings of a colleague would be dealt with later. Plus, it was Jack Piper, a friend I had covered hundreds of news stories with and I knew he would be happy to get the mike logo of his station in front of the camera along with mine, and I knew the magnetic power of the camera would turn Carver's full focus to my questions.

"Charlie," I began as I stuck my microphone in front of his face, "I know this has to be very disappointing for you. Do you think there's any way this can be changed by a higher court?"

"Oh definitely yes," Carver replied with more dejection than confidence. "We believe there are several reversible errors made by the State and the court that we can use in an appeal."

"Such as?"

"First of all the tape," Charlie answered, as if I struck a raw nerve. "We don't think the judge should have allowed the tape into evidence. That was strictly a work product protected by the lawyer-client relationship."

"Charlie," I switched direction, "when did you begin to get concerned in the trial that it might not go your way?"

Without any hesitation he said, "When the tape was allowed into evidence. We began preparing Linda then that the trial might not turn out in her favor."

The station gave me a free reign over the length of the live shot. No one back at the station feared viewers switching from the scene at the courthouse to watch another channel or calling to ask why we were preempting their favorite soap opera. This ten month odyssey to justice was the greatest soap opera ever seen in Southeast Texas. It had more unlikely plot twists and turns than any fictional soap operas. There was no fiction here. Five of the main characters were not written out of the script; they were killed in a cold, methodical murder and left in a shallow grave. This was riveting television. It was the end to the area's longest nightmare.

I literally waded through the mob of reporters, wires, camera lights, tape recorders, and microphones outside the courtroom interwoven through a mob of friends and family from both the Phillips and Linda, courtroom addicts, and just plain curious people wanting to be a participant in an historic moment. I did a walking and talking scene transition as I got myself and the camera in position to interview McGrath. He was clearly feeling the ecstasy of victory. He still wore his bulldog grimace but with a cocky smirk added. The emotional pitch of the scene was intense and it went up a notch higher when our blinding camera light hit McGrath. Along with the bright light there was a much smaller, much dimmer, but much more significant, red light. The red light was on, it was show time and McGrath was ready for his close-ups.

"Jim, I just talked to Charlie and he says he's confident they can overturn the death sentence."

"That's just lawyer talk," McGrath shot back with a smirk. "Of course they're going to say something like that. I would expect them to say that. There aren't any holes in this case."

"You're confident it will hold up no matter how far the appeals go?"

"Yes. No doubt," he answered as if assuring all the voters in Jefferson County that he had permanently put away a monstrous menace to society.

"And the tape, are you sure the admission of the tape will stand up in an appellate court review?" It was great TV but not necessarily my best moment as a reporter. I felt like a softball pitcher gently tossing a slow pitch to the plate to set up the batter. McGrath was standing there waiting and prepared for every question and ready to knock it out of the park for a home run.

"Oh yes," McGrath said without the slightest hesitation. "Every letter of the law was followed and the tape was properly admitted into evidence. It will stand up in an appeal. I have no concern it will be overturned."

"What about appeals? What about parole?" I tried to be as dramatic as possible but he was thoroughly enjoying being beamed live into the middle of prime daytime TV and into the middle of living rooms all over Southeast Texas. "Do you think Linda May will ever walk the streets of Jefferson County again?"

Without missing a beat he curled out his lower lip, looked directly into the camera, shook his head from side to side and shot back, "Not as long as I'm the district attorney of Jefferson County!"

CHAPTER FOURTEEN

The Interview

Before packing up our camera and live shot equipment I went back to Carver and asked about Linda. I figured it was a long shot, but I wanted an interview with her. There were two reasons I thought I had a good chance. I knew she liked to talk and secondly I figured she would probably want to give her side of the story. Carver would not commit but said he would speak to her and get back to me. I asked him to keep the interview idea under his hat and not tell any other media.

Unfortunately, Sharon Englade of the *Beaumont Enterprise* had the same idea about an interview as well which blew my chance for an exclusive story. Carver talked to Linda, they both agreed, and he arranged the interview for us the next morning at ten.

The ten o'clock interview meant I would have a story on the six o'clock news that night and the paper could possibly get it in the evening paper if they held up their presses and pushed everything back to accommodate the story. That meant deliveries to homes would probably be pushed back as well. More importantly, the rest of the TV and radio stations would just get to watch and listen in envy. I was feeling quite pleased with myself. For a reporter, there is nothing like a scoop.

The next morning Sharon and I met them at the courthouse. With Carver beside her, we set up our camera and lights in the same courtroom where the trial took place. I was there with the new $45,000 video camera the station had just bought for the production department. The camera was so valuable that this was the first time they let it be used by the news department. Along with Sharon was an *Enterprise* photographer with the usual assortment of 3 or 4 cameras, pockets full of film, and an array of lenses and camera bodies hanging all over him and stuffed in his photographer's vest pockets.

In spite of all that had transpired and all the gruesome testimony I had heard, it was good to see Linda again and sit down across the table from her. She wore a simple, plain, polka dot dress. Instead of one of the wigs, she tied a scarf over her head and over her ears covering her gray-streaked straight brown hair. She was in much better spirits and smiled and said a genuine 'good morning' to me and then to Sharon. Although it was only ten o'clock Sharon was thinking deadline and tried to goad us along in getting the lights set up and everybody wired up for the interview. It did not help that the $45,000 camera also came with a production photographer instead of a news photographer. Because the production department was so possessive of their brand new, ultra-expensive camera, Mike, one of the production personnel, was the photographer. Mike was comfortable making commercials with cars and trucks, or shooting produce for the weekly specials at one of the local supermarkets. He was not accustomed to news, or mass murderers. His hands were trembling so noticeably as he tried to pin the lavaliere microphone on Linda's dress that she commented about his tenseness saying she would not bite him. He laughed nervously, and with his hands still trembling, dropped the lavaliere in her lap, putting him in an even more embarrassing situation. She handed it back to him and he managed to finally get it clipped it to her dress without dropping it in her lap again, or worse, down the front of her dress. While Mike continued to set up, Linda, Sharon and I exchanged pleasantries and non-specific chit chat.

With audio levels checked, and all the lights set at just the right angles, and Sharon chomping at the bit, we started rolling the video with our interview. It was Linda, her attorney Charles Carver to the right of her, and Sharon and me on the opposite side of a table about 3 feet wide. It was the same table she had sat with her attorneys throughout the trial.

"How do you feel this morning about all that has happened since last summer?" I started the interview. Not a real hardball question I will admit, but I was not too concerned because I knew my biggest problem would be editing the interview down, not asking question after question trying to get something to use. Plus, I knew Sharon was a fantastic and more experienced reporter and would help make it a quotable and substantial interview. Linda was very calm and also apparently well coached in her response.

"I think it's just a matter of time until it's corrected," she began. "I know in my heart that I'm not guilty. I think the people did what they think was right. I don't feel any bitterness towards those twelve jurors. The jury's verdict probably would have been the one I would have given if I had been sitting in court listening to the evidence they presented. The jury felt they were protecting our county. I feel sorry for them. It's just a matter of time before the truth is known and I'm released. I have no doubt."

"Four weeks ago, I accepted Christ," she said explaining her confidence. "We have been having prayer services every night in the jail. This morning Sandra Washington and I were singing church songs. It's for God to judge us, not other people."

My mind was whirring and I could feel Sharon's disbelief as well. That tape of her intricately describing the murders was played before God and everyone. I wondered about Linda's sanity in thinking studying the bible and saying a few fervent prayers was going to make this all go away. Everyone believed justice was served. From the trial everyone heard how she had coldly, calculatedly, and carefully plotted out, then carried out, the murder of five innocent people. Nobody was saying she got railroaded, a dirty deal, or that it was a miscarriage of justice. Everyone I talked to — including people on the street who just came up to me and started talking about the trial — was in total agreement that Linda got exactly what she deserved.

"I don't feel bitter towards anyone," in mid sentence Linda's faced changed to anger as she continued, "except Joe Dugas. He's an animal. He's insane and should be killed. There's no doubt in my mind. If they had let Joe out, he would have killed me. No woman will ever walk off from him alive. He has no feelings towards people. He's going to kill again. There's no doubt in my mind."

"It's been like a nightmare," she continued. "For the first time, maybe, I'm waking up from this nightmare, this twilight zone," she said referring to the time that began when she and Joe met. "If I had walked out on him there's no doubt in my mind that me and perhaps my family would have been killed."

"If you feared him so much, why didn't you do something back then?"

"My only crime was not having enough courage to report Joe. I didn't have enough trust in the law. Even the day Joe was arrested and I was interviewed by the FBI and sheriff's office I came within a hair of going to the Nederland Police Department and saying, 'I've got problems. Help me. If I had, maybe I wouldn't be on death row."

"What do you intend to do while the case is on appeal?" I asked.

"I'm going to finish my schooling and get my high school diploma, learn more about the law, and study the *Bible*." Then she paused, and for the only time during the forty five minute interview, she got emotional when she began talking about her family.

"I've been very truthful with my children. They know what happened and they have accepted my sentence." Her voice quivered

177

and she began to cry. "I'm telling them to look at this like mom is going off to college, a learning experience for all of us. I'm going to use *Job* in the *Bible* for my inspiration to deal with this. God gives me strength to deal with it. It's God's will and I'm accepting it."

She pulled out a facial tissue like the ones she had tucked away all during the trial. She wiped away the tears and continued. "I am confident; I know in my heart I am not guilty. There is someone else out here in Jefferson County who was the accomplice to the murders, and one day that person will be brought in and I'll be vindicated."

"Linda," Sharon broke in, "if you still maintain you're innocent, how do you explain what happened to the Phillips family?"

"Joe told me his brother and Neal were out there that night. It's just a matter of time until the sheriff's office picks them up."

"Okay," I said, "but what about the voice on the tape?"

"As far as I can say, that's not my voice. I was under hypnosis. There is no evidence to link me to the crime."

She was totally oblivious to the contradiction. Although the trial was over, I could almost hear Carver internally screaming in his mind, "Are you nuts?!" You just said it was you under hypnosis!"

At that point Carver leaned over to her and whispered some kind of legal advice to Linda. Neither Sharon nor I could hear but my camera operator turned his head and looked at me as if he wanted to say something.

Later, Mike asked me if I could hear what Carver whispered, because he heard it clearly through his headset. When I was told we would broadcast the entire interview in a special program Sunday afternoon I helped with the editing of the show. When I got to the part of Carver whispering, I turned the volume on the input knob way up so that everyone listening could clearly hear him say, "Don't get into a debate about whether or not you were involved."

So taking his cue and without going into details, she added,

"This was done by some back stabbers. What's on that tape is not true. I don't want pity. I just want the truth to come out."

"Linda," how do you explain what got you involved in the murders?"

She coyly redirected my question. "My only sin was adultery, not murder. I needed to go to the doctor more. Women who go through hysterectomy surgery need to go to the doctor and minister more during that time. You need to know who you associate with. You could be around someone committing a crime. If I had talked to someone I wouldn't have started straying from home and from Leo for the first time in my life. If I hadn't taken that turn, I wouldn't have been out with Joe Dugas and I certainly wouldn't be subjected to what I'm going through now. That was the first time I've ever run around. I opened up a Pandora's box when I walked out my front door."

"There's the automatic appeal," Sharon said, "then the possibility of others after that. How do you plan to deal with what could be a very long process?"

"I still trust the criminal justice system. I have faith in God and I know that the truth will eventually come out. I'm living for the appeals. I'm not going to sit there and grieve and let myself waste. Someday I'll be back here in the real world again. I'm not bitter about what happened; not even against the district attorney. If I can come back I'll even vote for him. We need a harder crackdown on criminals and crime. I know the D.A. was just doing his job."

That line burned into my brain and I could not wait to share it with McGrath. Sure enough, when he heard it he got a big laugh out of it. He understood the irony if Linda did not.

After about 45 minutes, including a couple of tape changes, Linda quoted from a poem to end the interview.

'"*Have faith and wait*," she said. "*That's how I'll get through.*"'

With that, Carver signaled the interview was over and he would not let her speak any longer. He and Linda got up and left.

Carver went back to his office, Linda back to her cell and out of the nice outfit she had chosen for the interview.

It took about 20 minutes to pack our equipment and get back to the station. I rushed the production crew as fast as I could. I wanted us out of the courthouse and all traces we had been there removed. I knew if the other stations got wind of the interview I would lose my exclusive, and all hell would break loose.

They did.

It did.

By noon the word had gotten around the courthouse about our interview. Not just reporters, station managers went ballistic. Judge Gist was even drawn into the fray as irate media people called him and demanded he release Linda from the jail to come down for an interview with them. I learned later from both Carver and Judge Gist that intense pressure was applied from all directions. Non media, but influential people, were calling on behalf of the radio and TV stations, some imploring, some demanding, that justice be served by allowing the other media outlets access to Linda. Both feeling the heat and surprised by the passionate force of it, Carver acquiesced and set up a second interview, this time a press conference, for two o'clock that afternoon. Unfortunately it blew our station's exclusive for the day. But I knew my interview was much better and much more personal and candid than you get with a dozen or more reporters firing questions at you. But even better, I had the luxury of spending the afternoon gloating that I had all day to work on my story and everyone else would be scrambling just to get snippets on the air by six o'clock. And to make it even better, for the big news conference that afternoon, she never repeated her comment about adultery. I was the only one who had that nougat on tape. And the next day it was front page news, in bold italics, a two inch high headline, "*My sin adultery, not murder.*" It was not only front page news; the story was the top half of the front page. I laughed and gloated as I read it because I knew every other paper and broadcast station was seething that they had gotten the rehearsed, better coached, and watered-down version of mine and Sharon's interview that had no big, headline-making comments. In the course of my radio and TV career, I had been burned many times and being on the other side of the equation was definitely much better than having to explain to a news director why somebody else got the story and I did not.

CHAPTER FIFTEEN

Linda's Letters

For a reporter in Texas a capital murder trial is a gift that keeps on giving because a death sentence carries an automatic appeal. It is a story that can drag on for years, which means you can pull out old file video, dust off the facts one more time, and maybe even get a road trip when the case goes through each step of the appeals process. For Linda, her journey through the legal process ended in her favor when the appellate court in San Antonio overturned her death sentence in 1980 and commuted it to life.

By then I had moved out of Texas to get my masters degree, then moved back to Beaumont to go to work for the TV station that had been my competitor. When I got back at my first opportunity I asked McGrath what happened to overturn the verdict. He said his office was first informed that the vote by the appellate court was 5-4 to uphold her case and sustain the death sentence. McGrath said that after a few congratulations and a little celebrating in his office, a second phone call came through informing him that one of the judges changed his vote. With the judge's flip-flop the decision then became a 5-4 ruling to overturn her death sentence and commute it to life.

Following more than a year on death row, Linda began serving her life sentence at Gatesville in the Texas State Penitentiary system. I corresponded with her for several years after the trial and every year bought a subscription for her to an inspirational magazine, *The Daily Word*. In her lengthy, hand-written replies she thanked me and told me she was avidly reading her *Bible* daily and holding prayer sessions with other inmates. She fanatically believed in *deus ex machina*, the hand of God would reach down and get her out of prison. He had to because she was innocent, she was right, and the truth, will finally prevail. Later in her letters she also came up with a conspiracy that involved a well known state senator as the person behind the murder of the Phillips family, and also her incarceration.

Each letter came with a small piece of paper in the envelope with these words in red letters: GENERAL INMATE CORRESPONDENCE • TEXAS DEPARTMENT OF CRIMINAL JUSTICE — INSTITUTIONAL DIVISON.

As of this writing Linda is 62 years old and still in prison. In the mid-90's she wrote me saying she has had several strokes that have left her with lingering health problems. In her letters she has never wavered from being an innocent victim of circumstances and had nothing to do with the deaths of the Phillips family. Still reaffirming the statement she gave in the interview with me after her conviction and death sentence, she clung to the belief that the person responsible for helping Joe would be found and the truth would eventually be known, vindicating her of any wrongdoing. She still had faith and was waiting for the truth to come out.

Since her trial neither McGrath nor any other Jefferson County District Attorney has investigated the case any further, making the chances of anything new coming to light very doubtful. At this time, as far as the district attorney's office is concerned, justice is served, the case is closed, and there is no justification for any further investigation. She wrote me that there have been some private citizens who have tried on her behalf to get a rehearing on her case, but nothing has ever made it to the courtroom.

In Texas a life sentence carries with it a minimum of twenty years imprisonment before there is any possibility of parole. Since she was first put in jail, Linda wrote me that she has become a born again Christian, gotten her high school G.E.D., and worked extensively in the prison library system translating books into Braille for the blind.

In the first few years after her conviction, and even after her sentence was commuted to life, she was upbeat and confident she would be out, either through her case being overturned, or through parole.

In one of her letters she optimistically and in upbeat spirits wrote, "Keeping a clean record, and working, plus going to college has paid off for me. Little did I know all of the extra hours I worked, taking mess from other inmates and not fighting back would help me now. God sure helps us deal with problems and then renews our lives with hope.

"I work in the commissary, been there over a year, before the commissary I was in the laundry office, before that I worked in Braille. At this time I am a clerk. This unit has over 700 inmates. Having a job in the commissary is one of the top jobs on the unit. TDC (Texas Department of Corrections) believes in me as a person to go by all rules. Maybe in time others (free world) will also see me in the same light."

This letter was written 12 years before she would be eligible for parole. But at the time her case was under appeal and there was a chance she could be out in six months if her case was overturned.

As the years began adding up so did the toll of being in prison. She was a petite woman, not in any way physically intimidating, a characteristic that works against you in prison. In 1992 she wrote, "As for me I'm doing better. Had a physical breakdown the end of July. The doctor said I had been pushing myself too hard, plus the anemia played a part in it. I lost feeling in my left side, had problems with my speech also. After weeks of bed rest I was able to go back to work. However, I've still got a light problem with my speech, and if I overdo things the left side (arm - hand - leg) gives out on me. The body hits an exhaustion level and just closes down as I now know."

Part of her exhaustion came from just going to the hospital. It was not the prison hospital; it was the John Sealy Medical Center in Galveston. Every trip involved at least an eight hour process including a 250 mile back-road, two lane, bus ride from central Texas to the Gulf Coast, all the time handcuffed to another sick inmate, multiple strip searches, as well as other emotional and dehumanizing degradations, then repeating the process in reverse to go back to the Mountain View Unit in Gatesville.

Then in 1994 she wrote, "Due to health problems I've slowed down a great deal. The trips to the hospital, the surgeries, plus the two strokes have changed my outlook on many things. Freedom doesn't seem to be something I'll ever have. Guess all I want now is for the truth to come out, it would help my children and grandchildren deal with all they have gone through, and still go through due to my being in prison.

"I've been sick for months, on medication, had surgery, face more surgery. I just returned Saturday morning from the hospital and will go back soon. Plus I've been a little down mentally which doesn't help. I'll be okay in due time or go on with my Father, where there will be peace. If God has me to live, it's for His cause not my own."

Then in September of 1998 she wrote, "Only a note to let you know what I have been told about my parole. Carver told my sister I will never make parole.

"Please do not renew *The Daily Word*. It will not be needed in the future. Good-bye Roger. I'll not be writing again."

She did not give any specifics or reasons, just goodbye, adios, no más.

Then three months later, I got a Christmas card and this

note. "I went before the Parole Board September 16, 1998. On Friday December 11, 1998 the warden called me into her office. The board gave me a set-off (no parole) until when, I don't know. My heart broke in two. After 20 years of going by every rule of TDCJ, (Texas Department of Criminal Justice) putting up with the other inmates even beating me, taking my commissary, and having few visits, the hardest slap in the face - to know I must stay here longer."

And that was the last I ever heard from her. Following her wishes, I never wrote back after her letter saying she would not be writing any longer. She was in the Mountain View Women's Correctional Unit at Gatesville.

A trial is only a very small slice of a person's life. I do not know what happened in the decades before the murders that led Linda to standing over a grave, holding a rifle, and shooting four adults in the head. You can not listen to a trial without getting involved. In every trial I have ever sat in, there were moments when the state would be getting down to the nitty-gritty, itty-bitty details of how the crime was committed and I would catch myself thinking, *"Why did they do that? That was stupid. They should have..."* and then my eyes would go shut, my head literally pop backwards slightly as I snapped back to reality and realized, *Wait a minute I'm plotting a crime in my mind! Why would I do that?*

Like everyone else, there have been times when it was not safe for certain people to walk down the streets of my mind, and like everyone else, I've had some angry mental confrontations. We all do when we think we've been done wrong. We mentally fuss and fume, get mad and get over it. But why did Linda and Joe follow their anger from a fantasy to fulfillment? *Why didn't that anger stop somewhere? Why did their mental pictures end with the ultimate in retaliation, the murder of five innocent people? Why did they so intricately devise a murder plot that involved purchasing army camouflage fatigues, eye-black, and carrying out a dress rehearsal of the crime? What is the difference between me and a person behind bars?* I have made my share of poor choices in life. As I have sat in many trials thinking about how to commit a crime, why is it I snapped out of it and the people on trial let it stew and seethe in them until the mental pictures were acted out?

Why have my less-than-enlightened choices ended with fines, apologies, and an extra work detail in the Air Force, while Linda and Joe's ended with incarceration? It was because I never stepped over the line from a mental vision to physical violence. And this trial helped me to see you do not make that decision all at once. With a different decision here, a different choice at another time, it can be a very thin line between thought and action.

CHAPTER SIXTEEN

Joe Dugas

After Linda's trial the attorneys for Joe Dugas got a change of venue and his case was tried in Nueces County. The county courthouse is in Corpus Christi, a city about the same size as Beaumont and about 200 miles farther south on the Texas Gulf Coast. Besides the excitement of covering the trial, it also meant a road trip for me. Coincidentally, our station owner lived in Corpus and had a condo on the beach and that is where I stayed during the trial. It was great. It would have been better except that I was married for less than a year and I grew up on the southern end of Padre Island, which I considered much nicer than the Corpus Christi beach. Fortunately, there were also courthouse friends and workers there so paling around with them and enjoying the fresh gulf seafood made the stay more tolerable. I took my jogging shoes and did have some nice moon-lit jogs on the beach with the sound of the surf filling my ears and the sweet smell of the salty mist coming off the breaking waves. The view of a full moon rising from a condo 12 stories up overlooking the Gulf of Mexico was a nice perk too even though I did have to look at it by myself Friday, Saturday and Sunday nights, when I would have rather been back home in Beaumont.

Joe's trial sounded a lot like Linda's. Most of the facts and evidence were the same. The main difference being that there was no precedent-setting confession under hypnosis. But that did not matter to the D.A. at that point. McGrath already had Linda's conviction. He got it on his home turf, where he wanted it. He did not care that Joe won a change of venue. He knew, and was confident; he could convict him anywhere, any time, with any jury. He knew Joe had a very public record of misbehaving that would bring any jury anywhere to loathe him. Joe was — as the cops say — a 'bad act.'

Joe had no socially redeeming characteristics that might sway even one lone juror to be sympathetic. McGrath had several witnesses, including relatives, to call to the stand to testify about incident after incident of Joe's life-long lack of compassion for any living thing, physical abuse, and death threats. That, coupled with more witnesses testifying to his violent temper, gave McGrath a hand full of aces to play. Who is going to have sympathy for a guy who threatened several times to kill his own mother … his brothers … his wife … his in-laws … strangers in bars? Joe's attorneys, Bruce Smith and Sonny Cribbs, joked during the trial that they would consider it a major victory if the jurors even got up and went to the jury room to deliberate instead of just standing up at the end of the trial and saying, "He's guilty. Can we go now?"

Even 200 miles from home, when Joe's record was put on public display, a jury in Corpus Christi could rest easy knowing that no one in Jefferson County would be upset with them for taking this guy off the street and sentencing him to death or locking him away — forever.

The trial for Joe went much quicker because the State did not have to set up the links and go through all the legal maneuvers to get the hypnosis tape into evidence. The venue was different but the results were the same. A Nueces County jury, in less than two weeks, convicted Joe of capital murder, and like Linda, sentenced him to death by lethal injection.

After his trial I went back home and Joe went on death row at the state prison in Huntsville, where he remained until June of 1983. In 1980 I left KBMT, the station I was working for, and moved to Washington D.C. to get a masters degree. I got my masters in October of '81 and then accepted the senior reporter position at KFDM, my former rival station in Beaumont. June 20, 1983, I went out on an assignment and came back to find the newsroom in total chaos. Everyone was in a frantic mode, talking in half-sentences, making very little sense, barking instructions into the two-way radio, and scrambling to get reporters and cameras to some crisis in progress. After about five minutes I was finally able to piece together bits of information. I discovered our television station had just been sold to a group of newspapers including *USA Today*, and oh, by the way, Joe Dugas had been shot and killed. Wayne Sparrow, who had been my competition and nemesis five years earlier but was now a good friend and coworker, was sent to Livingston to cover the killing.

It happened as Jefferson County Investigators Pat Hayes and Russell Landry were transferring Joe from the county jail back to death row at the State penitentiary in Huntsville. What seemed to be just the temperamental personality of Joe turned out to be quite an elaborate scam. First Joe struck a deal with McGrath to give a deposition in one of Linda's appeals. McGrath and Landry went to Huntsville to take his deposition but Joe balked, refused to talk, and told them they would have to get a bench warrant to make him appear in court. It seemed like another instance of Joe being a jerk, but it was part of a very intricate and well planned escape attempt that he had plotted out while sitting on death row.

McGrath had no choice other than to get a warrant if he wanted Joe's testimony. So he got the warrant and brought him back to the county. However, after getting the free ride, Joe changed his mind and completely reneged on his end of the deal, refusing to either cooperate or testify. Or as they say in Southeast Texas, Joe 'crawfished.' There are crawfish in every stream and bayou along the Gulf Coast. They look like a miniature lobster. When a crawfish gets in a jam, it flips its tail under itself, propelling it backwards before a predator can get it. Joe 'crawfished' big time on McGrath and probably felt pretty proud of himself for doing so. He did have reason for feeling a little smug, he had used the system to get off death row for a few days, an all expense paid trip back home, and he got to see some scenery with colors other than the prison-gray of Huntsville's concrete walls. Plus, it gave him the opportunity to put his 'master plan' into action.

The prosecution has very little leverage with a person on death row because there is nothing you can threaten them with that is worse than the situation they are already in. So when Joe dug in his heels and refused to cooperate, McGrath had no choice except to fuss and cuss and send him back to Huntsville. It was during that trip that Joe made his last attempt at proving that he was really as bad as he tried to convince people. And with nothing left to lose, for the first time, he showed he had the guts and the brains to act on his own.

When finishing up this book, I talked to Landry, now 83 years old, and he recalled how he was the beginning of Joe's problems and ironically, the end as well. When Joe was first picked up in connection with the Phillips family's disappearance, he was interrogated for three days by the Anahuac County Sheriff's Department, FBI agents, and Texas Rangers. The fourth day he clammed up and would not talk to anyone.

Landry had a reputation of being able to get confessions out of suspects when no one else could, so he was called in. As he explained to me, "I'm not a religious fanatic, but I always prayed before I met with a suspect, and God would direct me in what I should say to get the person to confess."

Landry went in that Sunday morning and sat down with Joe.

Joe would not say a word. Again another irony of the trial, Landry's sister was an accordion player at the Rodair Club, Joe's home away from home, and he was very familiar with Landry's sister. Landry started talking about her and the Rodair Club and Joe began to respond a little. When he started opening up about the Rodair and Cajun music, Landry went 'full Cajun' on Joe and started talking to him in French. At that point he started to really warm up to Landry. After more loosening up, Landry started talking about the crime. Landry said Joe told him, "It seemed kind of like a dream to him and I explained that is often the case when a person has done something so bad that the mind can't accept it, so the mind tries to block it out."

For three days various law agencies tried every trick in the book to get a confession out of Joe. Landry told him, "I don't want you to confess. I'm not here for a confession, Joe. Just show me where the bodies are." After three days of no luck, it only took Landry about an hour to get Joe to take him to the grave site.

When Joe agreed to take him to the grave, Landry told Joe, "Now don't be like my wife and tell me I should have turned there or some other place after we've already passed it. Tell me before we get out there exactly where to go so we don't waste a lot of time."

Joe took Landry and several Anahuac County Deputies out to Highway 365 in mid Jefferson County. They drove up and down the road a few times but Joe could not remember the exact spot. Landry said, "As he tried to find the grave, Joe said Linda told him to look for a sign and the number 13. After a few passes there was a break in the fence and Joe said that looked like the spot. I looked just a few feet away and there was a highway mile marker sign, number 13. This was the first any law officer knew of Linda and it was the link that led to her arrest the next day."

In a slow, Southeast Texas drawl, Landry explained to me how it happened, "Once we got out of the car, he took us to an area where he thought they had buried the bodies but neither Joe, me, nor any of the sheriff's deputies could find the grave. Then a deputy saw a shiny, new twenty-two caliber shell casing on the ground. He called the rest of us over, and we found more casings. As we walked around the area near the empty cartridges, we discovered a soft spot on the ground. We brushed back the pine needles and saw where the dirt had been dug up. It was so well camouflaged even Joe couldn't find it."

Being an experienced crime investigator, Landry took only one investigative tool with him, a rod to stick into the ground. Landry told me, "I stuck it in the ground about three feet. When I pulled it out it had the distinct retched smell of rotting human flesh."

With that, Landry thanked Joe and then told the deputies to lock him up. It was not until Landry spoke those words that Joe realized he had just signed his own death certificate. Landry did not need a confession. He had the evidence. Because of the bond Landry formed with Joe in jail, Joe trusted Landry up until that moment. Then when he realized he had been played for a fool, Joe hated Landry from then on. Later he even filed a $1.7 million dollar lawsuit against Landry in Federal court for tricking him. Joe lost that case too.

After Joe's refusal to testify against Linda, McGrath had no recourse other than to transport him back to Huntsville. Landry and Hayes were chosen to do the job because Landry was familiar with Joe's case and would know the meaning of anything Joe might say enroute, down to the slightest nuance of any single word, phrase, or vague reference Joe might inadvertently utter. Hayes was chosen because he had a female inmate to interview at another prison after they dropped Joe off.

The three of them rode in Landry's personal car with Landry driving, Hayes riding in the passenger seat, and Joe in the back seat. Once again intuition worked for Landry. Joe kept sniffling and putting a handkerchief to his nose, like he had a cold. Landry thought he was up to something, so Landry made up the excuse that he needed to stop for a restroom break. He pulled the car over at a gas station in Livingston, a little East Texas town about an hour outside of Huntsville. It was a small town gas station that is off the main route and pumps a cheap brand of gasoline. And it was the kind of station where inside hanging on the wall, you will usually find a single key to their use-at-your-own-risk, one-room-serves-all, filthy restroom behind the station.

This was the first time I had heard the intimate details of Joe's death so I listened intently as Landry continued in his slow, precise account. "I got out and went to the restroom. When I came back I told Joe he was going to ride up front with me, and Hayes would move to the back seat so he could watch Joe. Joe refused to get out of the car. I reached in to drag him out when Joe pulled a shank."

I had never heard the term until Joe's death. I learned that a shank is prison slang for a piece of metal or anything that can be sharpened to hold an edge or a point, filed so sharp it can be used as a weapon to slash or stab someone.

At that point Landry said events began to happen very fast. "What I didn't know was Joe's right hand was free. It wasn't until after he stabbed me with the shank that I saw the unlocked handcuffs dangling on his left wrist. Joe had the shank in his right hand, and he stabbed me. I recoiled violently, and I hit the back of my head on the car door frame and Joe came after me.

"I remember Joe came out of the car and started wrestling with me trying to get my gun. He had me in a headlock. I was seeing stars and dizzy. I got to my gun first and when he saw me pull it out, he took off running and jumped over a wooden fence behind the station.

"Hayes ran around from the other side of the car when I pulled the shank out of my chest, threw it on the ground and took off after him. Joe apparently hurt himself jumping over the fence because when I came around it, and he made a lunge at me, his leg gave out. I got off two shots. The first hit him in the neck, the second was a body shot that killed him. He would have killed us both. He already hated me because he thought I betrayed him. And he had no love for Hayes either."

An investigation by the Polk County Grand Jury determined Joe had very cunningly planned the entire scenario while sitting on death row. By forcing the county to transport him he got outside the prison walls. The investigation uncovered that for $100 he had bought a handcuff key from a jailer in the state penitentiary. He stuck it up his nose for safekeeping until the time was right for him to blow or pull it out of his nose and unlock his handcuffs so that he could easily slip out of them at an opportune moment.

When he was checked out of the Jefferson County jail, he had two finely-honed shanks hidden inside a book. The official investigation determined that Joe made his shanks from the metal wire that bound the mop head to the handle of a mop in the Jefferson County jail. Joe had managed to get it off the mop and bend two pieces into a "J" shape. Holding the doubled end, he had a piece of wire about four inches long extending from his hand. He then took the extended end of the shank and rubbed it on the cement floor of his cell until the blunt end was worn down into a four inch spike that he could use like an extremely sharp, ice pick. Once he had them sharp enough to use as a weapon, he hid them in a book he had brought with him from prison. That is how he got them past his strip search on the way out of the county jail.

It was a really good plan except that luck was with Landry and not Joe. First, if the shank had been a millimeter or two longer, he would have instantly killed Landry. The shank went through Landry's liver and touched his heart. If it had penetrated his heart, Landry would have been killed on the spot. Secondly, instead of continuing to stab Landry and disabling him, Joe might have had time to get to Landry's gun. But Hayes was running around the front of the vehicle and Joe did not have that luxury. It was then a life or death situation for all three of them. Joe was already a convicted murderer, so if he got to Landry's gun he would have killed both of them. If not, one of them would shoot him. Fortunately Landry had enough strength left to get to his gun first, a .357 magnum, a handgun powerful enough to shoot through a car engine.

Like so many other uncanny events that helped convict Joe and Linda, and seemed to be a running theme throughout their trials, just two weeks before Joe's transfer, Landry bought his .357. The first time he fired it was to kill Joe. But fate also stepped in at that point as well. With the new gun Landry needed a new holster. The only holster for a .357 the salesman had was a shoulder holster. Landry, a veteran law officer of more than two decades, had always worn his gun on his belt until he bought that shoulder holster. When Joe stabbed Landry he started running his hands all around Landry's waist looking for his gun. It was the split second he spent looking in the wrong place that allowed Landry to reach up under his coat and get to his gun first. Joe was so intent on getting the gun that he did not notice Landry reaching up under his coat for the gun holstered near his armpit.

The story would have had an entirely different ending if Landry had still been wearing his belt holster. If his gun had been on his belt, Joe would have gotten his gun, killed Landry and Hayes, and taken off on a wild spree until killed or captured again. It was a bold move that would have put Joe in the league of the all time truly shrewd and daring criminals, and in the Texas bad guys' hall of infamy.

Landry told me, "Hayes and I both had brand new Three-Fifty-Seven's. We had a couple of boxes of ammo for them and I always carried a sawed-off shotgun and boxes of double-aught buckshot in my trunk. If he had killed us he would have been armed to the teeth with enough guns and ammo to take on anybody."

I knew both Landry and Hayes for years before the incident. I talked to them many times. My opinion, and their reputations, was that they were honest and capable law officers. When I first heard it I thought Joe's attempted escape story was a little too convenient, but personally knowing them kept me from going down the conspiracy route to a contrived escape attempt orchestrated by the

District Attorney's office.

A lot of questions were raised about the incident. It just had the slight odor of 'something ain't right.' Even people I'd run into on news stories who thought Joe was guilty, told me they felt the entire scenario seemed a little too unbelievable or convenient. However, the investigation by the Polk County grand jury cleared Hayes and Landry of any wrongdoing and ruled they had acted totally appropriately under the circumstances.

As we talked about all the events around Joe's death, Landry described his experience with the grand jury. "When I got through testifying the foreman and several members of the grand jury got up and shook my hand. The women on the panel hugged me. The foreman said they did not need to talk to any more witnesses, they knew the story. And they didn't talk to anyone else after me."

In the inquiry the investigators found the mop Joe used to make his shanks. It was in a cleaning closet in the Jefferson County jail, with a section of the wire mop-head binder missing. The investigators also found a worn spot on the floor of his cell where Joe had rubbed the wire, giving it a razor-sharp point.

The general attitude afterwards was that it was a shame that Landry came so close to dying and that a lawman was injured in the line of duty. However, although a few people thought the story was a little fishy, almost everyone was okay with the way the story ended. Instead of the cost of years of feeding him and expending more county money on appeals trials, two .357 slugs were a very economical resolution of events. After all, the state was eventually going to kill him anyway. Why draw the saga out any longer? He got his fair trial. Hang him and let the devil deal with him.

I remembered witnesses throughout both Joe's and Linda's trials testifying that Joe seemed to spend his whole life hurting people in hopes of giving him that swagger and aura, as well as reputation of someone with nerves of steel who should never be messed with.

When I heard the news Joe was dead, brought down by a

lawman's gun, I thought, *Well he's finally got it. Murdered five people, attempted escape from prison, outwitted and stabbed a law officer. It was just the kind of exploits that will make him a real bad ass to his peers, his cellmates on death row. A tough crowd to impress, but his was quite an impressive trail of documented violence. Posthumously, but he got the reputation he wanted so badly.*

And the death of 3-year-old Jason Phillips, who never again rode his rocking horse, is finally avenged.

Epilogue

James McGrath

Until his death James McGrath was incensed by the cruelty of the murders. In 1994 I talked with him and asked why he was so determined to get a conviction against Linda.

"Because of the brutality of it and I felt she was the one that was almost entirely responsible," McGrath said still firmly believing justice was served. "Without her it would never have happened. Joe thought of it but then he backed out. He didn't have the guts to do it. She pushed for it."

"Did you ever think during the trial you might not get a conviction?"

"I guess I did. It would have been possible if he (Judge Gist) hadn't let us get the tapes in. We could of lost it."

"Was she under hypnosis on the tape?"

"That's what they testified to."

"Did you ever look at Charlie Neal as a suspect?"

"No."

"So you think the scenario of Joe and Charlie Neal committing the crime was just the defense trying to put up a smoke screen?"

"Yes. We never took it seriously."

"Do you think she'll ever be paroled?"

"I don't think so. I don't think she'll ever get paroled. I wrote a strong letter before I left office that she never be paroled. That's my recommendation."

Charles Carver

Sixteen years had passed and Charles Carver was in the process of closing out his legal practice so he could move into the county courthouse when I called to ask him about his recollections from the trial. He said he could not give me much information as he is still bound by attorney-client restrictions. I asked if he thought the defense still had a chance when he joined the team.

"When I signed on they had already selected one juror," he said. "She was the wife of a Beaumont police detective."

This was another extremely curious legal decision by Howell and Erwing. The Beaumont police were heavily involved in the investigation and the wife of a detective would very likely know all kinds of inside information about the crime. She would almost certainly have very opinionated ideas about crime since it represented the main threat to her family's peace of mind. She would in all probability be the last person another lawyer, including Carver, would have picked, not the first.

"And the tapes had been discovered by the district attorney's office. With the tapes in evidence there was no way we could win."

Carver was leaving his legal practice to become a judge. He won the general election and was taking over the bench of Judge Larry Gist's 252nd Criminal District Court. Carver is now Judge Charles Carver and presides over the court where he defended Linda May.

Judge Larry Gist

In 1994 Judge Larry Gist retired from his criminal court position. Judge Gist still works for the county, presiding over a special court set up to handle only drug cases. This special court was created because of the heavy volume of drug cases in Jefferson County. Jefferson County sits on Interstate Ten on the Gulf Coast, making it the shortest route from the Mexican border to all points east in the U.S. Because of this strategic position the county has a lot of drug traffic passing through the area in addition to the everyday home grown drug activity on the streets.

Bill Howell and Helmut Erwing

Bill Howell and Helmut Erwing went back to their law practices in Houston and never tried another case in Jefferson County. Neither Howell, Erwing, nor Carver represented Linda during her appeals. For her appeals Linda had a court-appointed attorney because the attorney fees for her first trial exhausted all of Linda and Leo's savings and other assets.

Linda May Burnett

Linda May Burnett is serving a life sentence for capital murder at the Murray Unit of the Texas Department of Criminal Justice in Gatesville, Texas. She is now in her sixties and will be eligible for parole again in 2016.

Made in the USA
Coppell, TX
16 April 2022

76695112R00115